PRAISE FOR THE CODEPENDENCY CONSPIRACY

Dr. Stan J. Katz is a nationally recognized expert in the field of family relations, child abuse, and substance abuse. His past affiliations include the National Institute on Drug Abuse, Children's Hospital in Los Angeles, and the Graduate School of Social Welfare of UCLA. In addition to his private practice, he is Clinical Director of the Maple Center, Beverly Hills' community mental health center, and is a member of the Expert Panel for the L.A. Superior Court.

Aimee E. Liu was an associate producer of NBC's *Today Show* before becoming a full-time journalist. She is the author of *Solitaire* and the co-author of numerous other books and articles on business and health.

Other books by Dr. Katz and Ms. Liu include *The Success Trap* and *False Love and Other Romantic Illusions*.

CODEPENDENCY
THE
CONSPIRACY

HOW TO BREAK THE RECOVERY HABIT AND TAKE CHARGE OF YOUR LIFE

DR. STAN J. KATZ AND AIMEE E. LIU

WARNER BOOKS

A Time Warner Company

Copyright © 1991 by Dr. Stan J. Katz and Aimee E. Liu
All rights reserved.
Warner Books, Inc., 1271 Avenue of the Americas, New York, NY 10020

 A Time Warner Company

Printed in the United States of America
First Trade Printing: May 1992
10 9 8 7 6 5 4 3 2 1

Library of Congress Cataloging-in-Publication Data

Katz, Stan J.
    The codependency conspiracy : how to break the recovery habit and take charge of your life / by Stan J. Katz and Aimee E. Liu.
        p.   cm.
    Includes bibliographical references.
    Includes index.
    ISBN 0-446-39377-0
    1. Co-dependence (Psychology)   2. Codependents—Rehabilitation.
I. Liu, Aimee.   II. Title.
RC569.5.C63K38   1991
616.86—dc20   90-50532
                                                                          CIP

Book design by Giorgetta Bell McRee
Cover design by Rich Rossiter

For the Maple Center Staff and counselors;
how fortunate we are for their "codependency"!

—S.J.K.

This one's for Christina and Amelia.

—A.E.L.

ACKNOWLEDGMENTS

The authors gratefully acknowledge the important contribution Jamie Raab has made to this book. She has served as our shepherd and champion, giving freely of her insight, encouragement, and unswerving commitment to the ideas and principles contained in these pages.

Once again, we have Richard Pine to thank for the initial spark of excitement and confidence that got this project off the starting blocks. We are grateful also to Arthur Pine and Lori Andiman for their diligence on our behalf.

And finally we thank Debra and Marty for their love and support, now and always.

CONTENTS

CONTENTS

INTRODUCTION

Problem:

• Every time he drinks, he gets abusive. He swears and throws things. Sometimes he hits me. And yet he acts like a prince when he's sober. I love him, and I'm terrified of losing him, but I don't know if I can live like this much longer.

• My daughter and I are constantly at each other's throats. I badger her a lot to bring up her grades because I can't stand to see her flush her future down the drain. All I want is for her to be happy, but last night she called from a friend's house and said she's moving out for good.

• I hate being fat. I've tried every diet you can imagine, and once I actually got within five pounds of my target weight, but I always end up putting it back on. I guess I just love food too much—but it's making me hate myself.

• I can't stop thinking about him. I want to spend every minute with him, and when we're apart I worry that he's in trouble. The worst of it is that I've followed him and caught him with other women, and he won't even say he's sorry.

• I do my best work when I'm high. Cocaine makes me feel

great and gets me motivated, but it's already cost me all my savings, and my lover is threatening to break up if I don't quit.

• I have this thing about my closets. They have to be perfect. I clean them three times a week and have every shelf labeled. If I find anything out of place, I go crazy and start accusing everybody in the family. I'm afraid this is a symptom of some terrible neurosis.

Possible Responses:

1. Ignore your problems and maybe they will go away. (But the pain won't allow you to ignore them.)
2. Seek professional therapy. (But that's expensive and you can't be sure the therapist will really understand you.)
3. Try to solve the problems on your own. (But that hasn't done you much good so far.)
4. Join a self-help group. (People who have the same problems can relate to your pain, and most self-help groups are free.)

When you're lost and don't know where to turn, the loudest, most compassionate voice you hear is probably the one you'll follow. In America today, that voice belongs to the self-help movement. Whatever the nature of your pain, there is bound to be a group of people with similar problems who, having helped each other, are eager to help you, too. Because they've been there, they assure you, they will understand what you are feeling, as well as the problems you are experiencing in your daily life. They promise to offer empathy, comfort, and reassurance without blaming or judging you, and, through their example, you will gain the courage to dig deep down and uncover the source of your pain. Above all, you won't be alone any more.

Unfortunately, the most alluring voice is not always the most helpful. Self-help groups may entice you with reassurance, acceptance, and validation, but few offer real solutions. They do not promote full recovery. They promote dependency under the guise of recovery. And many are more concerned with proselytizing than they are with the real needs of individual members.

In my practice as a clinical psychologist I have worked with hundreds of drug and alcohol abusers, molested and abused children and adults, perpetrators, and families in crisis. I know the anger, pain, fear, and shame that addiction and victimization can cause. I also know that many individuals and families are enormously resilient and that many more can develop the resilience to completely recover from even the most tragic or profound crises. Yet such resilience is undermined by self-help programs that teach members to view themselves as powerless and disease-ridden, by "recovery experts" who maintain that virtually our entire society requires lifetime treatment.

In recent years, I have seen a marked increase in the number of my patients and patients of my associates who are members or veterans of self-help programs such as Alcoholics Anonymous and the related "Anonymous" organizations. Some of these patients joined the groups on their own, while others were referred by therapists who had endorsed the programs without fully questioning their value or validity. In many instances, the patients' original problems were exacerbated by their self-help programs. Additional conflicts were often caused by the policies or dynamics of their groups.

Before going any further, I should make a distinction between the organizations that I call self-help groups and those I describe as mutual support groups. The two terms are often used interchangeably, so that mutual support sessions for cancer patients are lumped together with self-help groups for people who spend too much money or "love too much." This ignores some crucial differences between the two approaches. Specifically:

• Mutual support groups generally are designed to help members deal with a specific problem or life transition, such as the death of a family member, but do not encourage lifelong membership. Most self-help groups instruct members that they must attend the group for the rest of their lives in order to maintain the recovery process.

• Mutual support groups frequently are supervised by individuals trained in leadership skills, who ensure that every member has an equal opportunity to share their problems and opinions and that the most vocal members do not monopolize the group or antagonize other participants. Most self-help groups are led by nonprofessionals and may prohibit professional involvement. Often the only qualifications for leadership in the self-help movement are membership in the group and familiarity with the group's program.

• Mutual support groups allow members to share their experiences and offer personal feedback but do not impose blanket prescriptions or behavior programs. Most self-help groups, conversely, prohibit personal advice giving but teach members that their recovery depends on their adherence to the group's program or beliefs (often the Twelve Steps used by Alcoholics Anonymous or a variation of the Steps).

• Mutual support groups encourage members to view their problems in the context of their lives as a whole and to believe in their capacity for complete recovery. Self-help groups teach members to view their lives in the context of their problems and to relinquish the notion that they can ever achieve complete recovery.

When people come together for the simple purpose of consoling, listening, empathizing, and sharing experiences, the results can be magnificent. These, after all, are the hallmarks of friendship, that vital, healing connection that has become so rare in today's rushed and anxious world. True mutual support groups do not pretend to offer anything more than friendship, and that is their great strength.

The groups that I refer to in this book as self-help groups have a far different agenda. Their mission is to help members change themselves, but only by embracing a prescribed set of beliefs and behaviors. Recovery that occurs by any other means is dismissed as self-delusion or denial.

The self-help movement began with the founding of Alcoholics Anonymous in 1935, and for some people who are truly addicted to chemical substances—the people for whom AA was founded —this approach may be their best means of salvation. But the movement today encompasses as many as 15 million members whose problems range from drinking and eating to shopping and worrying too much. Many of these people are *not* true addicts. They are people with problems who need guidance and support and acceptance, but they are not powerless. They can recover completely. They can achieve self-reliance. For these people, self-help programs may provide the best way to begin the recovery process, but in the long run they may do more harm than good.

Of course, this is not what you will hear if you attend a self-help meeting. According to the movement's leaders, virtually everyone needs to be in a self-help program because everyone, theoretically, suffers from the same chronic disease, a cross between addiction and victimization more popularly known as codependence. Self-help experts insist that, because this is a disease, it is not your fault if you are codependent. Because it requires treatment, you are powerless to control it on your own. And because it is chronic you can never put it behind you. The healing power of the group theoretically will enable you to bring your sickness under control, and as long as you stick with the group's program you can keep on top of it. However, if you leave the group or abandon its program, you will relapse.

Such "treatment" may make you feel good, but it can limit your options and alienate you from the people and opportunities you most need to help you reclaim your life. It works like symptomatic medication, making you feel and function better as long as you follow the prescription but never really resolving the underlying ailment.

My objective is to show you how to move beyond both your problems and the limitations of the self-help approach, so that you can complete the recovery process. This book picks up where most self-help programs leave off.

The first section details the benefits, limitations, and dangers of self-help groups, both for members and their loved ones.

The second half presents an eight-point plan to help you move beyond the "codependent," "addict," and "victim" labels and on to self-reliance. You'll learn to put your life back together, to come to terms with your problems in a way that allows you to move beyond them, and, finally, to establish the preventive measures that will keep you from backsliding.

One final word: Throughout this book I refer to cases that give testimony both to the dangers of self-help programs and to the tremendous healing powers that reside within us all. By condensing these cases into a few pages I do not mean to minimize the recovery process. It can be extremely difficult to change feelings or behavior. The transition may take weeks, months, or even years. Sometimes the process cannot be completed without professional help. But I hope that the suggestions and examples in this book will persuade you that recovery does not have to be a life sentence, that for most of us it is an attainable goal.

Some people lean on pain because it's all they know or all they feel they can count on. But you don't *have* to live with pain. And you don't have to surrender control to feel better. If you are ready to eliminate the pain and take back control of your life, you are ready to move from self-help to self-reliance.

THE
CODEPENDENCY
CONSPIRACY

PART I

The Codependency Conspiracy

CHAPTER 1

Behavior As a Disease

An addiction is anything we are not *willing* to give up.[1]
—ANNE WILSON SCHAEF
When Society Becomes an Addict

A kind of hysteria surrounds the issues of addiction and victimization in American culture today. The root of this hysteria is the belief that any behavior, situation, or relationship that causes problems or discomfort can—and should—be treated as a progressive, life-threatening disease. The vehicle for this hysteria is the vast network of self-help groups that has expanded in the last twenty years to include everything from critical problems such as alcoholism and child abuse to annoying habits such as excessive handwashing and junk collecting. (The National Self-Help Clearinghouse in New York has actually received inquiries about a group for people who "drink a little too much but not way too much Coca-Cola."[2]) The message of these groups and the books and articles that promote them is, ironically, that we cannot help ourselves but must rely on a combination of God, therapy, programmed instruction, and others with similar afflictions to show us the path to survival. Full recovery is impossible, say most of these groups, because our disease can recur at any time; we can never completely free ourselves or own our own lives.

I believe that this universal disease theory is both wrong and

3

potentially harmful to the millions who are in real pain and look to the self-help movement for real support. It holds that our vision should be limited to getting by "one day at a time" and that anyone who has ever been over- or underweight, had premenstrual mood swings, used alcohol or drugs, been divorced or hurt in love, or known the upheaval of emotional insecurity must always be on guard against a recurrence of this condition. The typical self-help message is that we will forever be haunted by the past, that the best we can do is survive.

My purpose in writing this book is to demonstrate that we do *not* all need to spend our lives under the shadow of former experiences, relationships, and behaviors. Complete recovery *is* possible. But before we can shake off the assumptions planted by the self-help movement, we have to understand how and why most human problems are different from diseases.

WHAT IS A DISEASE?

The medical and mental health professions historically have recognized two general categories of diseases:

Physical ailments or sicknesses are identified by rashes, fever, or other specific physical effects on the appearance and functioning of the body, and by the microbes, bacteria, or viruses that cause these effects. The disease model used by the self-help movement mimics this medical concept of disease as a condition caused by microbes, or agents beyond the infected person's direct control. In the self-help model, the disease has little or no relationship to the affected individual's personal values or beliefs. The diseased person is cast as a victim of the infectious agents, a person who is powerless over his or her disease and has no responsibility for its onset. The sickness is not viewed as a consequence of choices or actions but as something that *has happened to the affected individual*. While this model does accurately describe many physical ailments, it does not apply equally to mental and behavioral problems, which generally evolve in direct response to individual beliefs and values, actions, and choices.

The self-help conception of disease as a progressive condition does not even fit all medical illnesses. Some physical diseases, such as cancer, AIDS, and diabetes, are clear examples of progressive diseases. Unless arrested through treatment, they will usually progress to death. But other diseases, such as polio and tetanus, can be prevented through immunization. Still others, including many childhood diseases and common cold viruses, are self-limited. In otherwise healthy individuals, they rarely require treatment, and once they have run their course, many will never recur. Not all diseases are progressive diseases.

Mental or emotional disorders are identified by abnormal behaviors, thoughts, and feelings that interfere with an individual's ability to function. There are hundreds of different diagnoses listed in the psychiatric manuals, but the one common denominator to all serious mental disorders is that they are *outside the range of usual human experience*. The disagreeable and often painful feelings of anger, sadness, frustration, and regret that we all feel when faced with difficult situations should not be confused with disease.

Some mental disorders, such as retardation, schizophrenia, Alzheimer's disease, and some forms of depression, have a physiological component, which may be genetic or stress-related, and, in this regard, are comparable to physical diseases. Other mental disorders may stem from emotional trauma or abnormal conditioning (being raised in a war zone, for example, or in social isolation). However, it is extremely difficult and frequently impossible to pinpoint the causes of mental disorders. Sometimes the condition is caused by a combination of factors, and sometimes there simply is no identifiable cause. Also, the same circumstances that appear to prompt depression or anxiety in one person may cause no ill effects in another. Given the extreme variability of these nonphysiological disorders, it makes no sense to lump them together under a single diagnostic label or to apply the same treatment program to all of them. Some conditions are permanent or chronic, while others can be cured through behavioral training, psychotherapy, and/or medication. Still others are age-related and will simply disappear over time. The important thing is to match the most appropriate treatment to the individual problem, not to assume *a priori* that the condition is a progressive disease.

BEHAVIOR AS A DISEASE

The medical and psychological professions define addiction as a state of physical and/or mental dependence produced by the habitual use of a chemical substance, such as heroin, or a behavior, such as gambling, to attain a pleasurable sensation. People who engage in an addictive behavior without becoming dependent on it or who have quit the behavior for good are not addicts of that behavior. Habits that do not involve dependence and/or *are not outside the range of usual human experience* are not addictions. For example, we are all dependent on basic survival behaviors, including eating, drinking, and breathing, and most of us have certain pleasure-oriented habits, such as sex and socializing. But are these addictions? Of course not. They are not outside the range of usual human experience.

Many mental health professionals define addictions as mental and/or physiological disorders when the addict's craving for the drug or behavior becomes so uncontrollable that the need to satisfy the craving *prevents him or her from leading a normal life.* Unlike people with lesser habits, such as nailbiting, these addicts consume their drug or perform their behavior of choice compulsively and excessively, and direct their lives toward satisfying their craving even at the expense of their health, relationships, and, often, moral responsibilities.

But while it is important to distinguish the hard-core addict from the person with a less serious problem behavior, I do not believe that it is accurate or useful to equate addiction with disease. Remember, diseases are caused by infection, by outside agents over which the affected individual has no control. Therefore, the addict who becomes convinced that he has a disease also becomes convinced that he has no responsibility for his

6

condition; it was caused by outside agents—dysfunctional parents, perhaps, or poverty, or the pushers down the block. And since he had no control over the agents that caused his disease, what control does he have in quitting his addiction? Very little. Like a cancer patient, he will more likely rely on a treatment program that focuses on his "disease" than on his own self-determination and competence. But as vital as positive thinking and motivation are for the cancer patient, they are far more critical for the addict. Unless he has a sense of personal responsibility and commitment to self-reliance, no treatment program can guide him to complete recovery. Yet in accepting his addiction as a disease, he sacrifices these very strengths.

Medical diseases are not the same as addictions and addictions are not the same as problem behaviors, yet self-help leaders frequently use the terms "problem behavior," "addiction," and "progressive disease" interchangeably. Eating disorders, smoking, workaholism, gambling, promiscuity, substance abuse, and overprotective parenting all fall into this global category, which, we are told, is terminal. Writes Susan Cooley Ricketson, a Connecticut psychotherapist who specializes in treating codependency: "As you fall prey to addictions and continually live from a false self, you will eventually break down under the strain. Untreated codependency invariably leads to stress-related complications, physical illness, depression, and death."[3] The addict, in other words, is a passive participant, a *victim* of his own addiction.

Ricketson's statement reflects two assumptions that are fundamental to the self-help movement—and inherently flawed:

1. All addictions are progressive and irreversible, and they inevitably will worsen unless actively treated.
2. Any addiction will kill you if it progresses to its logical end.

The basic assertion that all addictive behavior is progressive is contradicted by the millions of people who simply decide to stop their problem behavior and do so without treatment. According to the American Cancer Society, for example, 95 percent of the people who quit smoking do so without any active treatment.[4] And while some researchers estimate that as many as a quarter of all freshmen college women are afflicted by the binge-purge eating disorder known as bulimarexia,[5] many of these young women return to normal eating habits in adulthood, whether or not they receive treatment.

My coauthor is one of these recovered bulimarexics. Between the ages of fourteen and twenty, Aimee Liu maintained a weight of between 90 and 100 pounds by dieting, exercising for hours, using laxatives, and vomiting. She was 5'7", a fashion model and honors student who fit the diagnostic profile for bulimarexic behavior to a tee. But this was the late 1960s, and few medical or mental health professionals were familiar with this type of eating disorder. Aimee was given innumerable tests to determine why she was not menstruating, but none yielded a diagnosis. Finally, midway through college, she began to emerge from her admittedly bad case of adolescent angst and came to terms with the many family, social, and sexual conflicts that had prompted her compulsive behavior. Within two years her weight was back to normal, and at age twenty-five she put this passage of her life to rest by writing about it in her first book, *Solitaire*.[6] One of the criticisms of the book by parents of bulimarexics and the professionals who were then beginning to treat the condition was that Aimee did not spell out a program for recovery or advocate a particular mode of treatment. In fact, she had never been treated or even attended a self-help group. By her own account, she had been a hard-core diet addict, and yet she claimed to have recovered simply by growing up. That was impossible, the critics said. But it is exactly how this syndrome plays out for many bulimarexics.

The evidence does not even support the progressive disease theory's blanket application to drug and alcohol abuse. Researchers who tracked the use of narcotics by Vietnam veterans found that half of the soldiers who tried heroin in Vietnam did not become addicted, and 56 percent of those who became heroin addicts spontaneously quit using it and remained abstinent after returning to the United States. Another 32 percent did report using heroin back home but did not become readdicted. Three years after coming home, only 12 percent of the Vietnam addicts had become readdicted. Contrary to the popular conception of heroin as a lifelong addiction, says Lee Robins, who conducted much of this research, spontaneous recovery is not the exception but the norm. He found that the average period from first to last use is nine years, and "recovery is nearly universal."[7] (This research was conducted before the advent of AIDS, which is frequently spread through the sharing of contaminated needles by intravenous drug users. Although AIDS has greatly reduced the survival rates for all IV drug users, Robins's conclusions about the duration of the addictive process are still valid.)

Dr. George Vaillant, whose book, *The Natural History of Alcoholism*, traced the drinking careers of 141 male alcohol abusers over more than thirty years, found that a kind of natural selection process occurred around age thirty-six, when many of the men who had had a drinking problem in earlier years either quit or returned to social drinking.[8] The number of what he called return-to-social drinkers increased with age. Michael Gazzaniga of Dartmouth Medical School maintains that drug abuse of all kinds declines with maturity. "After thirty-five," he says, "it just drops off precipitously."[9]

My own experience bears this out. During my three years with the National Institute on Drug Abuse (NIDA) training center in Los Angeles and two years as a consultant to NIDA, I conducted evaluations of drug and alcohol abusers in a wide range of treatment programs. Age was one of the key factors that determined whether an addict would succeed in quitting his habit. Another, which went along with age, was his motivation to quit. For many, the motivation came from hitting bottom and losing everything they cared about, including job and family. For others, it simply came from the decision that they no longer wanted to live the life of an addict. Either way, developing the motivation to quit took time, so that most of the men who succeeded in treatment were middle-aged or older. But once they were finally motivated, the type of treatment they received was largely irrelevant. They tended to succeed not because of a particular program or therapy but because they had *committed themselves* to quit using drugs and alcohol.

The same pattern shows up in studies of heroin addiction,

which report that most heroin addicts become users during adolescence or as young adults, and more than 90 percent are heroin-free by age forty-five.[10]

We see a similar curve among people who are drug and alcohol users but not addicts. As a member of the "baby boom generation," I have numerous friends and acquaintances who used drugs and alcohol heavily during the 1960s and early 1970s but quit as they got older and acquired more responsibilities, and as intoxication became less acceptable among their peers. *Rolling Stone*'s 1988 poll of Americans in this same age group—twenty-five to forty-four—showed that while 46 percent at some point in their life had used recreational drugs (the selection included cocaine, LSD, and heroin), about half of these former users had quit completely and another third had significantly decreased their drug use since the 1970s. The deciding factor in their quitting drugs was not treatment but maturity. "They have based their decisions on experience rather than prescription. . . . They may not want their children to try drugs, but they aren't going to tell them that sampling marijuana will turn them into lunatics. Not all drugs are equally harmful."[11]

Neither are all addictions. If we stick to the medical definition of addiction as behavioral or psychological dependence, then it is true that most addictions will lead to death if the addictive behavior is not stopped. But the self-help movement interprets addiction to mean *any* out-of-control behavior—or any behavior that we *perceive* to be out of control. By this interpretation, there are many nonlethal addictions. Marital infidelity, for example, is one variety of a "disease" that the movement calls sexual addiction, but unless your extramarital partner has a sexually transmitted virus or a homicidal spouse, it is not likely to kill you. It is also difficult to imagine death by excessive shopping, hand washing, loving, or taking care of others. Taken to extremes, any of these behaviors could interfere with normal functioning and might signal a very real mental or even physical disorder, but in themselves they are not lethal.

THE BOUNDARIES OF ADDICTION

One of the most common refrains in the self-help movement, as well as in advertisements for drug and alcohol treatment centers, is that addiction knows no boundaries; it cuts across all ages, races, and socioeconomic groups, just as a contagious physical disease does. If this were true, the level of substance addiction in the inner city would be the same as addiction in predominantly white suburban areas and would occur with equal frequency in both sexes and all racial and cultural groups. But social psychologist Stanton Peele persuasively refutes these assumptions, pointing out that:

• College graduates are approximately half as likely to smoke as nongraduates.[12]
• While moderate alcohol use is more common in upper income groups, people in lower socioeconomic groups who drink at all are more likely to be problem drinkers.[13]
• The highest rates of drug abuse consistently are found among disadvantaged, particularly minority, youths.[14]
• Women in general have from one-third to one-tenth the drinking problems of men, and the highest rates among women do not fit the stereotype of the middle-aged suburban housewife alcoholic but occur among young, unmarried, lower-class women.[15]
• Rates of alcoholism are extremely low in certain ethnic groups, such as Italian, Chinese, and conservative Jewish populations, which sanction moderate drinking but place a strong moral emphasis on self-control, socially acceptable behavior, and personal responsibility.[16]

This data indicates that addiction is directly affected by environment, education, personal beliefs, and values. Those who feel that they have a great deal to lose from addiction in terms of family and community support, financial security, health, and professional status, and who claim responsibility for their own behavior are the least likely to become addicted. Those who do not feel that they have much to lose and/or do not accept responsibility for their own conduct are the most likely to adopt the addict's role.

As I write this, the most celebrated drug case on the national scene involves Washington, D.C., mayor Marion Barry. After years of denying rumors of his cocaine use and lecturing the children of his community about the dangers of drugs, Mayor Barry was arrested on cocaine possession charges and, quickly thereafter, placed himself in a substance abuse treatment program to "heal my body, mind, and soul."[17]

At first glance, this case appears to contradict the point I just made. Certainly Mayor Barry had a lot to lose by using drugs, and especially by getting caught. Family and community support, professional status, and political power were all at risk. But the question remains whether *he* believed his drug use could cost him these assets and whether he accepted full responsibility for his behavior. His popular support among D.C.'s black community was so strong that shortly before his arrest, he was referring to himself as "invincible." His speedy retreat to a Florida substance abuse clinic helped him to save face and rally sympathy, but at the same time his lawyers were preparing to plead innocent to the possessions charges and were contacting publishers about a book telling the mayor's side of the story. His supporters were charging that he had been entrapped. Mayor Barry announced that he had "come to face my deepest human failures" and he subsequently dropped out of the mayoral race, but he did not say that he had done anything wrong, or even that he actually had a drug problem. He entered treatment, he said, because he sometimes drank too much. And the fact that he had spent the day of his arrest planning his reelection bid suggests that the only reason he admitted his "failures" was that he got caught. Judging from his conduct before and after his flight into treatment, his sickness was not caused by drugs but by the belief that his power and popularity would protect him. And they may well have done just that. Although Mayor Barry was convicted on one count of cocaine possession, he was acquitted on one other, and the jury failed to reach a verdict on the twelve remaining counts.

Addiction is simply not the same as a virus or bacteria that unexpectedly invades our bodies and takes control of our lives. Addictive behavior involves choice and consent. It is an active expression of our values, skills, and expectations—or lack of them. As devastating as the effects of chemical dependency, compulsive gambling, or other true addictions unquestionably are, the responsibility for the addiction lies with the addict. To blame the addiction on the abused substance or to call the addict a victim of his addiction is tantamount to blaming the messenger for news we would rather not hear.

THE FAMILY AS A DISEASE

In the 1940s the self-help group Al-Anon, which was organized by and for the spouses of alcoholics, began to spread the message that relationships can be just as addictive as substances and behaviors. Al-Anon was the first group to use the basic tenets of Alcoholics Anonymous as a program for relationship addicts. As it has since evolved, this theory of addiction-by-association, or *codependence* (also called codependency and co-dependence), encompasses not only the families of substance abusers but a broad range of parents, children, divorced men and women, widows and widowers, unhappy singles, and various combinations of these categories. Today there are self-help groups for all the different types of codependents, most of which are patterned after AA and Al-Anon.

Obviously, any relationship involves and generates certain types of behaviors—and vice versa—so there is some overlap between these groups and the ones dealing with problem behaviors. This is particularly true of groups that deal with substance abuse; members of AA frequently attend meetings for codependents as well. But relationship groups are more concerned with feelings than behaviors. And even feelings that are well within the range of usual human experience can justify attendance.

"Codependency," writes best-selling author and recovering

codependent Melody Beattie, "involves our responses and reactions to people around us. It involves our relationships with
other people, whether they are alcoholics, gamblers, sex addicts,
overeaters, or normal people. Codependency involves the effects these people have on us and how we, in turn, try to affect
them."[18] In other words, *any* human relationship qualifies as
codependence.

One assumption that is basic to the codependence movement
is that we learn how to relate to other people in our life—and
thereby acquire our sickness—by watching and interracting with
our parents. Hardly a new idea, this theme runs throughout
psychoanalytic theory, from Freud onward. Parents directly influence their children, guide their emotional development,
shape their beliefs. When a family is truly dysfunctional, that
is, unable to function within the range of usual human experience, it is likely to have a negative impact on all its members.
The standard analogy is to a mobile: when one piece of the
mobile is swinging wildly out of control, all the pieces react by
moving in ways that will offset the disturbance to the unit as a
whole. The major flaw in this analogy is that the pieces of a
mobile *only* affect and are affected by each other. They cannot
elect to drop off or join another mobile.

Very few families are as self-contained or limited as mobiles.
From an early age, most of us are affected by a constellation of
characters that extends well beyond our parents. Many child
development experts maintain that our beliefs are shaped as
much by our peers and teachers as by our families. Our culture,
including both our legal system and the media, largely directs
our moral conduct and the expectations we bring to our personal
relationships. Finally, while we all inherit certain traits and
tendencies from our parents, we are not their clones, nor are
we clones of each other. By analyzing its size, weight, and lo-
cation relative to the other pieces, we can accurately predict
the movement of a piece dangling in a mobile. We cannot
achieve the same kind of accuracy by applying such formulas to
human beings. We can spot patterns and make generalizations,
but there are always exceptions, and the patterns and generalizations change constantly.

THE "SCIENCE" OF CODEPENDENCE

In 1955, University of California psychologist Emmy Werner began a study that was designed to test the impact of early childhood conditions on long-range mental health and functioning. She and her team of researchers identified every child who was born that year on the island of Kauai, Hawaii, and then monitored the children's growth and development over the next three decades. Of the nearly seven hundred individuals in the sample, approximately one-third were considered "high risk" from infancy because they had experienced four or more of the following risk factors before the age of two: medical problems at birth; chronic poverty; physical or sexual abuse; parental illiteracy, alcoholism, abandonment, divorce, or mental illness.

Now, if we accept the basic theory of codependence, we would have to assume that all of these high-risk children would need years of therapy to recover from their traumatic youths. But, while Dr. Werner found that many did have some learning and behavior problems, she also found that fully one-third developed without significant problems—or treatment—into "competent, confident, and caring young adults. . . . Indeed, a significantly higher proportion of the high-risk resilient individuals than their low-risk peers rate themselves as 'happy' and 'delighted' with their current life circumstances."[19] Moreover, the thirty-year follow-up showed that the vast majority of high-risk children who had gotten into trouble in their teens, through delinquency or unwanted pregnancies, for example, managed to rebuild their lives during their twenties. "Risk factors and stressful environments do not inevitably lead to poor adaptation," concludes Dr. Werner. "It seems that, at each stage in an individual's development from birth to maturity, there is a shifting balance between stressful events that heighten vulnerability and protective factors that enhance resilience."[20]

Dr. Werner's findings reinforce a recent report on the codependence movement, funded by the National Institute on Alcohol Abuse and Alcoholism, which concluded that there is "no data at all" to support the theory that people can develop

15

a "personality disorder solely on the basis of their family membership."[21]

Nevertheless, scientific-looking diagrams, labels, and formulas are favorite tools of codependence theorists such as John Bradshaw, who also likes to summarize his conclusions in acronyms such as BAD CHILD, PERSECUTE, and CRISIS (each letter stands for a key point in his book *Bradshaw on: The Family*). These theorists override the exceptions to their rules by simply creating more rules, more versions of the codependence disease, more diverse examples of the afflicted. In a single diagram, Bradshaw presents fifty-three different roles to describe the ways in which family members may act out their codependence.[22] Many of these roles are contradictory. For example, a codependent "addict" may be an offender, victim, or rebel, and a child of a codependent may play the part of clown, overachiever, underachiever, or saint. Melody Beattie lists 254 separate characteristics, any one of which could theoretically signal codependency. This list, which she warns is "not all-inclusive," includes such critical indicators as "wish good things would happen to them," "think and talk a lot about other people," "get frustrated and angry," "get confused," "advise," "gauge their words carefully to achieve a desired effect." Beattie also includes contradictory characteristics such as "say everything is their fault" and "say nothing is their fault," "take themselves seriously," and "don't take themselves seriously."[23]

By creating so many different disease characteristics, the codependence leaders offer a slot for everyone. We all must be codependents because we all fit at least one of the descriptions. This tactic is very good for book sales and lecture attendance, as both Beattie and Bradshaw have discovered. As of February 1990, Beatty's book *Codependent No More* had sold more than 1.5 million copies. Bradshaw's *Bradshaw on: The Family* had sold more than 350,000 copies, and he was commanding upward of $6,500 per day for speaking engagements, plus all expenses and first-class airfare. But the tactic is also irresponsible. Most of the feelings and behaviors listed as codependence traits are perfectly normal. They do not indicate that we came from dysfunctional families or are in one now. They do not prove that we are addicts or that we have a dread disease. All they prove is that the authors of these lists have contrived a theory so broad, so multifaceted that it is virtually meaningless.

Another disturbing effect of the codependence movement is its reduction of grown men and women to "adult children." This term originally was coined by self-described adult children of alcoholics such as Sara Hines Martin, who writes: "The term adult children comes about not because we are offspring of alcoholics but because we are children emotionally."[24] Now, according to Rokelle Lerner, cofounder of Minnesota's Children Are People organization, you don't even "have to be the son or daughter of an alcoholic to be a co-dependent. Any critical parent will do."[25] The mere idea infantilizes grown men and women at the same time that it presents them as victims of their parents' thirty- and forty-year-old mistakes. "Embrace the child within you," the movement gurus advise. They do not tell you how to embrace the adult you must become.

The codependence movement misleads people trying to manage the ordinary, often vexing difficulties of everyday life and relationships into believing that their problems are much more serious (and glamorous) than they often are, and yet that they bear none of the responsibility for these problems. It offers too-easy excuses to people whose upbringings were, in fact, perfectly normal, and it gives false hope to people with truly dysfunctional histories who require more than self-help palliatives to heal their wounds.

WHY CALL ADDICTION A DISEASE?

The disease concept of addiction dates back to 1784, when Dr. Benjamin Rush first described habitual drunkenness as a disease. One of the signers of the Declaration of Independence and a pious Presbyterian, Dr. Rush also believed that lying, murder, and political dissent were diseases and that the cure lay not in judicial punishment but in bloodletting and abstinence. Dr. Rush's theory of drunkenness as a disease was seized and expanded upon by the temperance societies that eventually won

Prohibition and today stands as the basis for the modern temperance movement spearheaded by Alcoholics Anonymous.

Although it went out of favor during the less forgiving Victorian era, Dr. Rush's interpretation of all undesirable behavior as a disease was resuscitated during the past century by members of the psychiatric and legal communities. Karl Menninger, the psychiatrist for whom the famous Menninger Clinic was named, echoed Dr. Rush's beliefs when he wrote, in 1928: "The time will come when stealing and murder will be thought of as a symptom, indicating the presence of a disease, a personality disease."[26] Along with Sigmund Freud's earlier pronouncement that personality disease is caused by sublimated conflicts rooted in early childhood, Rush's and Menninger's theories form the foundation for today's codependence movement. The overriding presumption throughout is that the *individual* is unaccountable.

One of the foremost critics of the progressive disease theory of human behavior is Thomas Szasz, psychiatrist and author of *The Myth of Mental Illness*, who wrote: "Psychiatric diagnoses are stigmatizing labels, phrased to resemble medical diagnoses and applied to persons whose behavior annoys or offends others."[27] The reason we are so keen to slap a disease label on unwanted behavior, he argued, is that we have difficulty accepting or controlling it any other way.

Szasz ignores the serious mental disorders, such as mental retardation and Alzheimer's disease, that clearly cannot be blamed on the victim. He also downplays the real pain and disorientation that mental instability can cause. But his assessments of our culture's overuse of the disease label and the label's insidious danger are right on target. By fitting our problems into disease categories we create the illusion that they can easily be explained and treated without our ever claiming responsibility for them.

An unfortunate result of our culture's acceptance of the disease theory is that we tend to overlook cases of individuals who cure or avoid problems by claiming responsibility for them. Of the 106 million users of alcohol, about 88 percent never develop a drinking problem, and for every cocaine or crack abuser there are three or four others who have tried the drug without becoming hooked.[28] If we paid as much attention to moderation as we do to dependency, we might learn how to stop addiction at its source.

Instead, the media feeds our misperceptions about addiction by glorifying celebrities who have bottomed out, while ignoring or criticizing stars like basketball player Kareem Abdul Jabbar, whose 1983 autobiography revealed that he had used drugs moderately in college but never abused them or needed treatment. Instead of learning more about how celebrities who have tried drugs keep from becoming abusers, we are bombarded with the first-hand sagas of recovering addicts such as football player "Hollywood" Henderson, musician John Phillips, and actress Drew Barrymore, who were unable to control their drug use. The addicts have been turned into role models because they support the disease theory, while the examples of former controlled users like Jabbar are suppressed because they contradict it.

Another reason that moderate behavior is downplayed is simply that it does not demand attention. The actress who has a quiet glass or two of wine every night and wins an Academy Award makes headlines for her work, not her drinking. If instead she celebrates the completion of a new film by going on a binge and running her car up a telephone pole, it's her drinking that will make the news the following day. Behavior that is considered unusual, shameful, or threatening gets attention, while moderate behavior does not.

Unfortunately, the proponents of the progressive disease theory have a tendency to overlook this basic principle and make generalizations for our entire culture based on a pathological sample. George Vaillant observed that researchers who rely heavily on clinical reports frequently overlook controlled drinkers: "Clinicians tend to encounter alcoholics during periods of relapse. Alcoholics who return to asymptomatic drinking feel too well or too guilty to recontact the clinician. Nor, like many abstinent alcoholics, will controlled drinkers be reported to the clinician via the grapevine, as is true sometimes of abstinent alcoholics attending AA meetings."[29] Thus, the common assumption is that all alcoholics who do not abstain will relapse to uncontrollable drinking. Vaillant, however, found that approximately one-fifth of the alcohol abusers in his sample succeeded in returning to asymptomatic drinking—about as many as relied on abstinence for recovery.

The psychiatric profession's tendency to pathologize unwanted behavior is encouraged by the insurance industry. As anyone who has ever filed an insurance claim knows, few insurance companies will pay for treatment without a diagnosis. The rule applies equally to medical and psychotherapy patients. As a result, doctors in both fields routinely exaggerate patient complaints into recognizable diagnosis for the sake of the claim form. Unlike medical patients, however, the vast majority of psychotherapy patients do not suffer from pathological conditions. Most have garden variety problems, are experiencing a personal crisis, or are going through a difficult transition in their lives. I do not mean to understate their turmoil or pain, but what they are experiencing is not, by and large, disease. Yet that is what we therapists must tell the insurance companies if our patients are to get the help they need.

Most of us explain this distinction to our patients, but not all patients willingly accept it. On the contrary, some embrace their disease diagnosis for the same reasons that our culture has embraced the disease theory: it explains and validates problems that they cannot otherwise accept or control. Also, in a perverse way, it has become trendy to be sick. Frank Riessman, executive director of the National Self-Help Clearinghouse in New York, put it this way: "The social climate is such that it has actually become fashionable to be 'in recovery' from everything from drug addiction to spouse abuse."[30]

Although self-help group participation is generally cost free and therefore exempt from insurance pressures, these groups, too, promote the disease theory. Groups for "women who love too much" teach that unconditional love is an addiction, like alcoholism, which must be treated as a disease. Messies Anonymous teaches that messy housekeeping is a disease, Kleptomaniacs Anonymous that stealing is a disease, Compulsive Shoppers Anonymous that consumerism is a disease, and so on. The treatment for most of these diseases, however, involves no professional or medical therapy, only participation in the group.

THE SPIRITUALITY OF SELF-HELP

One key reason for the tremendous popularity of mutual support and self-help organizations is that they provide a sense of community. The desire for reassurance and a sense of belonging are common to us all. A place to be open and honest, to air grievances and desires, to meet others who have experienced the same problems and can help us come up with possible solutions is something we all need, particularly during periods of crisis or change. Mutual support groups generally perform these functions beautifully.

Most self-help groups, unfortunately, underscore the community spirit with dogmatic rhetoric and rules. At each meeting, members run through the "laundry list" of symptoms that are their common bond and proof of their affliction. They review the group's recovery program, then listen to each other talk about their struggles with the disease and their personal attempts to work the program. They are instructed to share their own feelings, but not to advise or admonish others. Instead, they learn to place their faith in the group and its program. AA and other Twelve Step programs teach that "unmanageable lives" are caused by "defects of character" that must be removed by God in order for the restoration of sanity, and that recovery requires lifetime membership in the group—even after members are "clean and sober." Group is not just a place, it's a permanent identity.

It is no coincidence that self-help programs and religious cults share the same "new age" stage. Both systems promise an antidote to the general alienation and loneliness of our culture, a substitute for families and communities that have come unglued. Both demand substantial offerings of time and devotion to their respective programs, and encourage reliance on the group for social, emotional, and practical support. While in cults the prerequisite for belonging is submission and the sense of community is predicated on collective devotion, in self-help groups the prerequisite is disease or victimization and the collective identity one of pain.

21

"They provide a sense of identity and direction to individuals. . . . Former dopers now 'turn on to God'; the promiscuous have become celibate; indolent drifters have become hardworking zealots." Cult expert Lowell Streiker is writing about cults in his book *Mind-Bending*, but his observations apply equally to self-help programs. Both types of organizations can produce highly positive results—and highly negative ones, as well. "For many individuals," observes Striker, "conversion marks the beginning of a spiritual quest which lasts a lifetime, and which takes them to ever higher and more integrative levels of existence. Unfortunately, the usual pattern is not one of growth. . . . Converts become very deindividualized. Their conceptual ability shrinks. Their speech becomes cliché-ridden. Their personalities atrophy. Instead of undergoing a liberating rite of passage, they appear trapped at an immature stage of development."[31]

This immaturity is reflected in the apocalyptic vision of the world embraced by self-help leaders such as John Bradshaw, who writes: "The crisis is not just about how we raise our children; it's about a hundred million people who look like adults, talk and dress like adults, but actually are adult children. These adult children run our schools, our churches, our government."[32] Ironically, the self-help movement's answer to the crisis is not to make these "adult children" more mature, but to encourage them to develop their child-ness. Embracing, loving, nurturing, talking to, and even taking the Inner Child for walks and car rides is a key component of the recovery program recommended by codependence leaders such as Bradshaw and Robert Subby, who encourages his fellow adult children to "sit yourself down somewhere in front of a mirror and imagine that the reflection you see is your own inner child. Look straight into his or her eyes and say: 'Thank you for not giving up.' "[33]

Like cults, self-help organizations serve up strong nontraditional religious messages and tend to regard those who dispute their program as hostile, unsaved, unenlightened, or, in the words of AA, "dry drunk." They view their program as *the* source of truth and enlightenment. The program obliges with prescriptions for behavior and belief, and plenty of spiritual jargon. Seven of AA's Twelve Steps specifically mention God, prayer, meditation, or spirituality, as in the Eleventh Step, which reads: "Sought through prayer and meditation to improve our conscious contact with God as we understood Him, praying only for knowledge of His will for us and the power to carry that out."[34] The writings of self-help leaders have similar religious overtones. "Through your spiritual awareness of a Higher Power," writes Cooley Ricketson, "you can begin to reclaim your inner reality and fill your world with meaning and love. I believe your longing for connection is a quest for life. To be fully alive you seek intimacy and connectedness with others, with a special partner, with God/Goddess and with your own heart." This is remarkably similar to the message of Baghwan Shree Rajneesh, who oversaw a commune of several thousand followers in Antelope, Oregon, in the early 1980s. The Baghwan's central message, as described by Frances Fitzgerald, who wrote about the commune in her book *Cities on a Hill*, was that "God was in all things, a living current of energy flowing through the temporary and illusory world forms, and that the Buddhas were those who saw through the illusion of self and of time to the great Oneness and Suchness of existence."[35] (The Baghwan's commune disintegrated when Rajneesh fled the country and several of his aides were convicted of attempted murder, wiretapping, immigration fraud, and arson.)

Cults and self-help programs maintain that salvation lies in the ability to give yourself up to a Higher Power. But the real key to salvation is not in relinquishing control to a treatment program or guru or your Inner Child. The highest power lies within your own fully developed self.

NOTES

1. Anne Wilson Schaef, *When Society Becomes an Addict* (New York: Harper & Row, 1987), p. 18.

2. Charles Leerhsen, "Unite and Conquer," *Newsweek* (February 5, 1990): 50–55.

3. Susan Cooley Ricketson, *Dilemma of Love: Healing Codependent Relationships at Different Stages of Life* (Deerfield Beach, Fla.: Health Communications, 1989), p. 13.

4. Stanton Peele, *The Diseasing of America* (Lexington, Mass.: Lexington Books, 1989), p. 25.

5. Jane Brody, *Jane Brody's Nutrition Book* (New York: Norton, 1981), p. 283.

6. Aimee E. Liu, *Solitaire* (New York: Harper & Row, 1979).

7. Lee Robins, "Addict Careers," in *Handbook on Drug Abuse*, eds. Robert Dupont, Avram Goldstein, and John O'Donnell (National Institute on Drug Abuse, 1979), p. 332.

8. George Vaillant, *The Natural History of Alcoholism* (Cambridge, Mass.: Harvard University Press, 1983).

9. Larry Martz, "A Dirty Drug Secret," *Newsweek* (February 19, 1990): 74.

10. Robins, p. 333.

11. "Portrait of a Generation: The Rolling Stone Survey," *Rolling Stone* (May 5, 1988): 57.

12. Peele, p. 160.

13. Ibid.

14. Peele, p. 159.

15. Peele, p. 70.

16. Peele, pp. 71–72.

17. Edwin Chen, "Barry Flies to Florida Substance Abuse Clinic," *Los Angeles Times* (January 23, 1990): A4.

18. Melody Beattie, *Codependent No More* (New York: Harper & Row, 1987), p. 26.

19. Emmy E. Werner, "High-Risk Children in Young Adulthood: A Longitudinal Study from Birth to 32 Years," *American Journal of Orthopsychiatry* 59 (January 1989): 72–81.

20. Ibid.

21. Beth Ann Krier, "Excess Baggage," *Los Angeles Times* (September 14, 1989): V1.

22. John Bradshaw, *Bradshaw on: The Family* (Deerfield Beach, Fla.: Health Communications, 1988), p. 83.

23. Beattie, pp. 37–45.

24. Sara Hines Martin, *Healing for Adult Children of Alcoholics* (New York: Bantam Books, 1989), p. viii.

25. Krier.

26. Melvin Konner, "The I of the Storm," *Los Angeles Times Magazine II* (October 8, 1989): 18.

27. Ibid.

28. Martz.

29. Vaillant, p. 219.

30. Leerhsen.

31. Lowell D. Streiker, *Mind-Bending* (New York: Doubleday, 1984), p. 30.

32. Bradshaw, p. 4.

33. Robert Subby, *Lost in the Shuffle* (Deerfield Beach, Fla.: Health Communications, 1987), p. 62.

34. Alcoholics Anonymous World Services, *Alcoholics Anonymous* (New York: AA World Services, 1976), p. 60.

35. Frances Fitzgerald, *Cities on a Hill* (New York: Simon & Schuster, 1981), p. 291.

CHAPTER 2

Victimization and Disease

Getting a divorce was the best move Nina had ever made. For eleven years, Patrick had berated and abused her. The first time he beat her was in Niagara Falls, three days after they got married. After that, his violence became a fact of life. He hit her more than two hundred times. Nina remembered them all.

It was her friends who finally gave her the courage to leave —her friends in the battered women's group she joined after one of Patrick's tirades sent her to the emergency room with a concussion. In group Nina felt for the first time that she was neither crazy nor trapped. After she described how Patrick had locked her in a closet all night, many of the women wept for her.

Through the group, Nina saw that her marriage was diseased. She loved Patrick too much. She gave away too much of herself without demanding enough in return. And Patrick took full advantage, perverting her love by abusing her. He'd turned her into an emotional cripple.

The group urged Nina to take Patrick to court and expose his crimes, because only when her pain was out in the open and he'd admitted his cruelty would she finally be set free. In the meantime, she needed to accept that she'd been victimized and stop cowering in his shadow.

One morning after Patrick went to work, Nina packed up her two children, moved in with a friend from group, and called a lawyer.

Patrick, of course, came to court with a full arsenal. He called her a liar and a hysteric. He claimed he'd never hit her without provocation and insisted he'd only done that a handful of times. Then his lawyer called their son, Jason, to testify against her. The thirteen-year-old told the judge that his father had never touched him or his sister, that his parents fought all the time but he'd never seen his father attack his mother first. He said that *Nina* usually started the fights, that she'd once bitten Patrick's arm so badly the wound required stitches. If he had a choice, said Jason, he'd like to live with his dad.

Nina exploded. She did her best to convince the judge that Patrick had somehow gotten hold of Jason and brainwashed him, but the judge awarded custody of Jason to Patrick. Five-year-old Stephanie would stay with Nina. The children were each to spend one night a week with the noncustodial parent.

I first met Nina three years after her divorce. Patrick had taken her back to court for refusing to allow him to see Stephanie in over a year. On the recommendation of Nina's attorney, the court had appointed me to evaluate the family and work with them to restore regular visitation.

In order to get both sides of the story, I asked to see the mother and son together first. While Nina told me the history of her marriage and divorce, Jason sat with his back to her and stared out the window. When Nina finished, I asked Jason to tell me if he had anything to add to what she had said.

He replied, looking me straight in the eye, "Half the time when she was screaming for Dad to stop hitting her he hadn't laid a hand on her. Dad's strict, sure, and he can be mean if you rub him the wrong way, but I'm never afraid around him."

"You see how he's been brainwashed," said Nina, shaking her head. "I feel sorry for you, Jason. You're an abused child. You're never going to get out of his shadow."

"Wrong, Mom. I'm already out. I have my own eyes and ears, and I have my own opinions. You're the one who's still living in his shadow. The whole time we're together, all you ever talk about is him! What he did. How terrible he is. How he's made you suffer. But Stephanie's the one I feel sorry for. I only have to listen to this shit for a few hours a week. She's got to live with it!"

"You hear that! This from my own son!"

"What I hear," I said, "is that Jason feels a lot of resentment toward you. Nothing to do with what happened during the marriage. He's angry about the way you treat him *now*. He feels like you're trying to take out your anger toward Patrick on him. Is that right, Jason?"

Jason nodded and blinked at the ceiling.

"Even if my children suffer, I have to take care of myself," said Nina, folding her arms across her chest.

"What do you think it would take for you to stop blaming Patrick?"

"How can I ever stop blaming him for what he did to me? He has left me with scars I'll carry for the rest of my life!"

After talking with Nina and Jason, I asked to see Stephanie and Patrick. Stephanie, aged eight, clung to her mother in the waiting room and cried as she entered my office. I managed to get her calmed down enough to let her mother leave, but she curled into a ball on the couch and refused to talk or look at her father.

I asked Stephanie why she was so angry.

"He hurt Mama," she mumbled. "I can't trust him until he apologizes."

These were not the words of an eight-year-old. Someone had been telling her what to think and say about her father.

"Stephanie," I said, "Has your father ever hurt you?"

"No."

"Are you afraid of him?"

"No."

"Do you think he loves you?"

Stephanie stared at her knees.

Patrick leaned forward, watching her from across the room. He looked hurt and tired.

"Stephie," he said, "don't you know that I love you, honey? Don't you see that's the reason we're here?"

"Until he takes responsibility," said Stephanie, and again I had the sense that someone had put words in her mouth, "nothing will change."

"Sweetie," said Patrick, his voice quavering with urgency, "your mom and I were not good together. I hurt her. She hurt me. I am sorry I lost my temper sometimes, and I'm sorry we stayed together so long. It was hard on you, I know, but I'm not some monster. I'm your father and I miss you. Don't shut yourself off from me."

Tears edged down Patrick's cheeks as he finished talking. Stephanie stared, as if trying to decide whether her father was putting her on. I gave her a box of tissues, gesturing for her to pass it to her father. She hesitated, then handed it over. When Patrick looked up she was almost smiling. At that moment Stephanie and her father took the first step toward rebuilding their relationship.

Following my assessment of the family, the court ordered weekly visitations and joint therapy sessions for Stephanie and her father. Nina was warned that she could be jailed if she interfered. Grudgingly, she complied.

About two years after I first met the family, Nina and Stephanie got into an argument while driving, and Nina made her daughter get out of the car. Stephanie walked the two miles home and began to pack as soon as she arrived. When Nina saw what she was doing, she began to shout at her. Stephanie grabbed a kitchen knife and threatened her mother to back off. Half an hour later, Patrick picked up Stephanie and took her home with him.

The next day, Nina was in my office, desperate to repair the damage. She still blamed Patrick for everything that happened, but she was now willing to concede that it wasn't enough to simply point the finger. For more than five years she'd been doing that, and not only had it not brought revenge, it had cost her her children.

My first question surprised her.

"Are you still going to those self-help groups?"

She nodded.

"What are they telling you?"

"Patrick's an addict. And his disease became my disease. I enabled him to abuse me by never standing up to him."

"It sounds like this group has intensified your connection to Patrick instead of setting you free. You now not only have the scars from his physical beatings but you have his disease."

She stared at me in disbelief, as if I were speaking blasphemy.

"Stop worrying about what the group would say or think," I continued. "Speak for yourself. What is it you really want? To punish Patrick? To be obsessed with things that happened twenty years ago? Or to free yourself of the past and recover your children's trust?"

Nina swallowed hard. "I want my kids to love me again."

"That's your top priority?"

She nodded.

"Why?"

She looked puzzled.

"Do you want them because you miss them? Because you don't want Patrick to have them? Because you're concerned about their well-being? Because you're afraid of being left alone?"

"It gets pretty complex," admitted Nina. "I guess I feel all those things."

"Good. Now we have a goal, and we have a realistic view of the situation. Those are the first two steps back."

"Back to what?"

"Back to self-reliance."

ARE VICTIMS DISEASED?

By insisting that addicts are rendered powerless by the disease of codependence, which in turn is rooted in victimization by toxic families, the self-help movement has thoroughly intertwined the concepts of victimization and pathology. Nina's self-help group, for example, had managed at once to validate her identity as an abused wife and to convince her that her inability to leave her husband was a symptom of illness. These messages saddled her with a double stigma. On the one hand, Nina was powerless to defend herself. On the other, her mistreatment was the result of her own sickness. Nina's personal responsibility and free will were simply not factored in.

Nina's case also illustrates how the term "victimization," like addiction, has come to describe incidents that were previously considered accidents, misunderstandings, or the normal ups and downs of life. In many ways, this is a positive shift. Domestic violence is now being taken seriously as a criminal as well as social problem. Rape and sexual molestation are now widely recognized as crimes of violence rather than passion or sex. Organizations have been created to protect the legal rights of victims in a justice system that often seems to favor the rights of accused criminals. These are all changes to the good. It is important to realize, however, that not all types of victimizations are equally damaging or traumatic.

When a violation involves serious emotional or physical trauma, it can lead to mental disorders, including chemical dependency. But the victim's personal perspective and state of mind frequently have an effect on the outcome that is equal to or greater than that of the violation itself. When sixty-nine-year-old actress Viveca Lindfors was slashed in the throat by a man wielding a razor in the streets of New York City in early 1990, she received twenty-seven stitches to close the wound, then proceeded on to her planned poetry reading and expressed sympathy for her attacker, who was later arrested. Certainly there are others who, in Lindfors's place, would have been debilitated by the event. The critical factor was not what happened but the victim's preexisting mental health and attitude.

Two other critical factors are the cultural context in which victimization occurs, and the beliefs and values of the victim. Assuming comparable and relatively minor physical injuries, a soldier who is shot during a foreign war is less likely to suffer permanent emotional distress than a target of a drive-by shooting in her own neighborhood. If the soldier believes in the necessity of the war, comes home to a supportive family and community, and receives a medal, the injury may actually boost his self-esteem. By contrast, if the drive-by victim is poor, gets little support from family and friends, and believes that she is powerless to improve her circumstances, her injury could very well spiral into severe emotional disturbance.

Unfortunately, in our eagerness to do right by all victims of all crimes, we often jettison our objectivity and ignore the variables, accepting charges of wrongdoing without question, exaggerating the severity of crimes, and demanding retribution at any cost. We treat any complicity on the part of victims as a sickness, just as we do their ensuing rage and shame, and shower them with sympathy without considering what they really need to reestablish an independent life.

CHILD MOLESTATION: NATIONAL CRISIS OR HYSTERIA?

Nowhere is our lack of objectivity more evident than in our reactions to reports of child molestation. The media portrays sexual abuse as a national crisis. Self-help groups for molestation victims are proliferating. And the nation's courtrooms are inundated with new allegations of abuse every day. But many of the lawyers who are charged with turning these allegations into convictions estimate that as many as 40 percent of the accusations are insubstantive.

Over the past fifteen years, I have conducted evaluations in hundreds of child-abuse cases, and I believe that physical and sexual abuse of children is a real and tragic problem. I vehemently support the protection of children and the prosecution of perpetrators. I do not, however, believe that there is a child molester lurking behind every rock or in every preschool.

Just how easily we can lose our perspective on this issue was brought home to me recently by three calls I received in a single week. The first was from a woman concerned about a seventy-year-old school-crossing guard. She told me she was worried that this man might be a child molester, because he winked at the little girls and called them "sweetheart." There were no other indications that this man would take advantage of a child, but she was alert and vigilant.

The second call was from a woman who was very suspicious about the sixteen-year-old boy who babysat for her children. She was concerned that his motives for babysitting might be devious.

The last call was from a divorced man who had shared custody of his three-year-old daughter. He was afraid that his ex-wife, with whom he'd had a bitter, contested divorce, would accuse him of sexual abuse to gain sole custody of the child. He said that he was afraid to kiss or hug his own daughter because it might be misconstrued by his ex-wife. He had read of a case in which similar allegations had resulted in criminal prosecution of a father and prolonged separation from his daughter.

These calls all reflect the witch-hunt mentality that has been fueled by widely publicized cases such as the one involving some four hundred children who attended McMartin Pre-school in Manhattan Beach, California. The calls also reflect the very real damage that this hysteria is doing to our communities and families. Ordinary people are being taught to view friendliness as depravity, to treat innocence with suspicion, to feel threatened by a smile. But most disturbing of all is the proliferation of child-abuse accusations in divorce cases, which vastly outnumber the sensationalized cases such as McMartin. The father who called me had reason to be concerned. Many of the allegations of child abuse by divorcing parents are purely vindictive—and extremely damaging to both the accused spouse and the children involved.

The Richie family is typical of the divorce/molestation cases that I routinely evaluate. Bonnie and Adam Richie had been married for ten years and had two children, aged three and four when the couple separated. Because of Bonnie's history of drug abuse and sexual promiscuity, the court awarded custody of the children to Adam. When Bonnie heard the decision, she threatened to kill her husband, and the judge issued a restraining order against her. Two days later, Bonnie filed charges against her husband for child molestation. The children were immediately taken away from him and placed in the care of Bonnie's parents—with whom she, too, was living.

Over the next year the children underwent numerous medical exams, not one of which turned up any physical evidence of molestation. The psychological evaluations, which Bonnie delayed until more than two months after filing charges, suggested that Adam had bathed the children, had allowed them into his bed when he was wearing pajamas, and that they used to play a game called circus in which he would sometimes hold them under the crotch while lifting them in the air, but they never played nude games. Evaluations conducted by licensed, court-appointed therapists did not corroborate Bonnie's allegations that her children had been exploited, that Adam was a "pervert" or a threat to the children. However, Bonnie's chosen therapist for the children was an unlicensed intern who conducted her initial interview by reading the children a booklet called "My Daddy Hurt Me." Each page of the booklet showed an illustration of a molestation scene with accompanying text such as "My Daddy strangled the cat" and "My Daddy brought in a group of men and they touched my private parts." Through the booklet, the children learned all the things that might have happened to them. All they had to do to indicate whether anything actually had happened was to point at the picture. When Betsy, the older child, pointed at the picture for "Daddy put his penis in my vagina," the therapist told her she was a very brave, good girl, whereupon Reuben, the three-year-old, pointed at the picture showing "Daddy put his finger in my anus," and he was complimented, too. Bonnie's case was built on the children's "accusations" during this and subsequent sessions with this therapist.

Meanwhile, the children did not see their father for more than six months. When the court appointed me to the case, I insisted on evaluating the children and father together without the mother present. Bonnie fought this for nearly three months, saying that the children were terrified of Adam, that he would brainwash them, that they would be traumatized for weeks before and afterward. When the meeting finally took place in my office, the children ran eagerly into Adam's arms. They demanded to know why he hadn't seen them, why he wouldn't return their calls (he had been prohibited from making any contact with them). They wanted him to come live with them, and they asked him to promise that he would never again leave them for so long. In short, they felt that he had abandoned them.

Betsy also wanted to know, "Why'd you take all our toys away and lie to the police?"

"Did you see him do that?" I asked her.

"No."

"Who told you these things?"

"Mommy," said the child.

When they left my office, Betsy and Reuben yelled, "Please come see us!" As soon as they saw their mother in the waiting room, however, their faces turned grim and worried. They knew that this was the expression Bonnie expected to see.

I am convinced that the Richie children believed that they had been abused. They had been taught that things had happened that were very bad but not their fault, and that they needed their mother to protect them. Their therapist taught them that they had been traumatized, that they needed a lot of help and a lot of time to get over what had happened to them. She also advised Bonnie and the court that Adam should not be allowed to see his children until he admitted that he had abused them and submitted to treatment himself.

Neither Bonnie, her therapist, nor the court considered the detrimental impact on the children of prolonged separation from their father, and Bonnie's personal history and the custody dispute were not considered to have any bearing on the child-abuse allegations. So, while the investigation dragged on, Adam was forbidden from seeing his children except during a single forty-minute monitored visit each week.

After two years, Bonnie's therapist was removed from the case and the children were assigned to a court-appointed therapist. The following year, the court concluded that there was insufficient evidence to show that the children had been molested or that their father was a danger to them. There was, however, sufficient evidence that Bonnie would try to sabotage the children's relationship with Adam as long as they remained in her parents' custody, and, for that reason, he was again granted custody. By now, though, the damage to the children was severe. Their trust in Adam had been shattered. They believed that he had abused them, that both parents had lied to them, and they felt abandoned. Having been taught by one therapist to think, act, and feel like victims, they would need years more with another to accept that it had all been a big mistake.

TREATING SURVIVORS

"Survivors don't ever get out of the role of having been a victim," writes social worker Cynthia Crosson Tower in her book *Secret Scars*. Neither do the children who go into therapy because a vindictive parent or a crusading prosecutor says they have been victimized. Neither do the adults who join groups such as Adults Molested as Children (AMAC) because they think that maybe they have repressed a childhood molestation that would explain the pain and anxiety they've been feeling. These individuals, whether children or adults, will be scarred for life, not necessarily by the abuse, which may have been extremely minor or never happened at all, but by the "recovery" process.

One way to mitigate against this damage is to adjust the diagnosis and treatment of victims according to the specific nature of the abuse. I do not think that a parent whose hand lingers momentarily while diapering his or her child belongs in the same category with convicted child pornographers or pedophiles, yet many therapists and self-help groups lump the victims of these different perpetrators together and treat them all as if they've been equally traumatized. If you don't remember feeling abused or distraught as a child, you may be told that you are repressing your memories when, in fact, you may never have had these feelings at all. If you were fondled at an early age by a close friend or family member, you may actually have enjoyed the experience. Simply because your therapist or self-help group interprets an incident as molestation does not mean that you ever felt abused. (Often molestation is identified on

35

the basis of the perpetrator's arousal alone, and the "victim" may not even have been aware that anything unacceptable was taking place.) And if you never felt abused, it's highly unlikely that your victimization caused you any lasting scars.

In my practice, I have found that sexual abuse victims generally fit one of three categories:

1. The victim behaves normally: has no nightmares, does not masturbate excessively or imitate sexually seductive behavior.

2. The victim's behavior suggests problems apart from the molestation: extreme fearfulness or aggression, emotional withdrawal, depression, all of which may signal feelings of abandonment, neglect, or other problems.

3. The victim's behavior suggests physical and/or emotional trauma directly related to the molestation: recurrent nightmares, sexually seductive acting out, excessive masturbation, complaints of genital pain, aversion to her/his own body and sexual behavior. This degree of traumatization is usually caused by fear, physical pain, and the perception that trust has been violated. It is most likely to occur as a result of incidents that:

- Take place within a violent or otherwise nonsupportive family environment
- Involve intercourse, digital penetration, sodomy, or oral-genital sex
- Are part of a pattern of abuse over an extended period
- Involve multiple perpetrators
- Involve explicit threats to prevent the victim from revealing the abuse
- Cause physical injury
- Occur during early puberty

Even with severe abuses such as these, however, not all victims are traumatized. For this reason, it is as important to look carefully at the aftereffects as it is to find out what actually happened during the incident.

If you were abused before you were six and you have never experienced or displayed any signs of emotional trauma, you may simply need to be reassured that you did nothing wrong and are not at fault. (Children who receive treatment for such early violations need to understand that no one should touch them in an inappropriate way, and they should be taught to tell a trusted adult if anyone ever tries to do this.) But such treatment usually requires only a few sessions. More extensive therapy and/or participation in a group that includes victims of serious abuse may distort your own experiences and get in the way of your recovery.

If the conflict you feel about your abuse is intertwined with other serious family or psychological problems, you need to focus on these problems separately in treatment, recognizing that the different problems may have little to do with each other, and that the abuse you suffered may have been relatively insignificant.

If you have been *severely* traumatized by an abuse, whether as a child or adult, you may require longer-term therapy to work through your residual feelings of humiliation and grief and to repair the damage to your self-esteem. In this case, a self-help group might help you to reestablish feelings of trust and belonging, particularly if you do not have a strong or supportive family. But remember that the goal of recovery is to interpret your past experiences so that you can go on to lead a normal, healthy life. Adopting the survivor/victim role as a badge of courage—regardless of how severely you were victimized—will not enable you to reach this goal.

ANCIENT WOUNDS

The more time that has passed since you were victimized, the more susceptible you will be to suggestion and distortion of the original events. Such distortion, simply a function of memory, affects sublimely happy recollections as well as painful ones. For example, when I was five years old I spent a summer holiday in a house on Lake Michigan. For years afterward, I remembered this house as a mansion, extremely luxurious and enormous. At age twelve, I returned and found that my mansion was just an ordinary lakefront cabin. The natural distortion, deletion, and misinterpretation of memory makes it an extremely unreliable basis for personal identity. Yet many of those who label themselves "adults molested as children" are pinning their adult identity on recollections no more accurate than my memory of that holiday cabin as a palace.

Many therapists and victims' groups unintentionally teach AMACs to exaggerate their memories of abuse, to believe that the violations were more serious than they remember. The assumption behind such advice is that anyone who claims to have been molested will try to minimize the incident rather than exaggerate it, denial and rationalization being typical expressions of shame. Unfortunately, this assumption can backfire with individuals whose abuse was minimal but who have other, more serious problems that they refuse to confront.

Clifford fit this description. On one occasion when he was six, Clifford was fondled by his uncle. After he first recalled the incident during counseling in his early twenties, his therapist suggested he join a self-help group for victims of sexual abuse. Clifford began attending group meetings once a week. By the time he started therapy with me, he was still in the group, had received counseling for more than eight years, and had never moved beyond his outrage at his uncle, now dead. I saw Clifford for more than three months before he finally agreed to look at the other aspects of his life. Only then did he reveal that his father had died when he was twelve, that he had a mentally retarded sister, and that he had had four affairs during his nine-year marriage—all with members of his self-help group.

As critical as Clifford's encounter with his uncle was, it did not occur in a vacuum and should not have been allowed to overshadow everything that happened before and after, yet because his identity as a sexual abuse victim was constantly reinforced by his former counselor and his group, it not only remained the central focus but automatically was blamed for everything that went wrong in Clifford's life.

I would never underestimate the pain and suffering caused by physical and sexual violence or the vital role of therapy for individuals who have been traumatized by these crimes. But when our definition of victimization becomes so broad that day-care workers are suspect because they hug or hold children on their laps, when we embellish the wrongs done to us in the past in order to excuse mistakes we are making in the present, it's a sign that our well-intentioned concern has gone awry. As a society and as individuals we need to guard against the impulse to brand every conflict or violation as a form of victimization and everyone who has ever been wronged a victim. We owe it to accused perpetrators, to alleged victims, and to ourselves.

CHAPTER 3

Labels That Help, Labels That Harm

The labels we use to define ourselves are extraordinarily powerful. They help to determine our relative places in society, the way others treat us, how we conduct our lives, and how we feel about ourselves. We have the power to choose our labels, and we have the power to change them.

I encourage my patients to define themselves in positive, constructive terms that emphasize their strengths over their weaknesses and enhance their self-esteem. The self-help movement, by contrast, generally teaches followers to adopt labels that accentuate their deficiencies.

According to John Bradshaw, "100 percent" of people today are codependent.[1] Likening our present society to Hitler's Germany, he writes: "We are in the death throes of an epoch."[2] Anne Wilson Schaef goes even further, provocatively asserting that "the number of co-dependents in the U.S. exceeds the total population. . . . I am talking about a whole system that has such elements as confused, alcoholic thinking (AA—Alcoholics Anonymous—calls it 'stinkin' thinkin' '), dishonesty, self-centeredness, dependency, and the need for control at its core."[3]

The movement's driving message seems to be: Assume that you are weak and sick because there is no chance that you can be naturally healthy.

My message is that these labels are inaccurate and serve no constructive function, either for individuals or society.

To demonstrate how insidious the labeling process can be, consider the following statement:

I am a/an _____

and the following possible responses:

adult	adult child
moderate person	addict
member of a family	codependent
professional	workaholic
strong individual	victim

Now look at this statement:

I am _____

and some possible ways to complete it:

capable	powerless
sane	insane
human	defective
loving	needy
normal	diseased

While the two sets of columns above may appear to contain opposite characteristics, there is no *objective* difference between the terms on the left and their counterparts on the right. Both columns in each set could describe the same person. The difference between the two is simply a matter of attitude and interpretation. The descriptions in the right-hand columns, all of which figure prominently in Twelve Step programs, intensify feelings of insecurity and low self-esteem. Those on the left, by contrast, highlight feelings of competence and high self-esteem. None of these labels are absolute. They are subjective assumptions, not facts.

HOW LABELS HURT

Ironically, while the self-help movement is promoting negative labels, most other popular movements are waging war against them. Civil rights advocates have worked for decades to eradicate ethnocentric labels (blacks are "intellectually inferior" to whites or "more athletic") because they distort not only white attitudes toward nonwhites but the way nonwhites view themselves. Feminists have fought a parallel battle against the traditional image of women as dependent and powerless, descriptions that the codependence movement is busily reviving. And educators are trying to stamp out comparative labels in the classroom because these labels have proven to be self-fulfilling prophecies. Kindergartners whose teachers tag them as bright, for example, tend to become high achievers, while those who are called slow generally evolve into poor students, *regardless of their actual aptitude*.[4] Children who are segregated into "learning disabled" groups tend to achieve less than those with equivalent learning difficulties who are mainstreamed in regular classes.[5]

From minorities and feminists to people with physical disabilities, there is consensus that negative labels are harmful because they encourage divisive stereotypes and restrict opportunities on the basis of a particle of an individual's experience or identity. Instead of defining ourselves in terms of pathology, we should be working to bring our lives into balance, heightening strengths rather than liabilities. Problems need to be recognized as *parts* of the whole rather than as total identities. There are critical differences, for instance, between having an addiction and being an addict; being victimized and being a victim; having a dependency and being dependent. Yet the self-help movement generally ignores these differences and per-petuates negative labeling.

DISEASED UNTIL PROVEN HEALTHY

Every one of us has negative as well as positive characteristics. One of the hallmarks of good health is the ability to recognize this complexity and establish a constructive balance. One of the hallmarks of poor mental health is the tendency to view oneself in the bleakest terms possible. Yet most self-help groups insist that the only way to deal with a problem is to adopt it as your primary identity. As a result, every one of these groups stamps its membership with an affliction, preferably one that works well in a catchy acronym or as initials. Adult children of alcoholics become ACAs, children of Holocaust survivors CHSes, victims of incest VOICES (Victims of Incest Can Emerge as Survivors) or AMAC (Adults Molested as Children).

One AA leader told his group, "If you think you have a prob-lem, or if you think you are an alcoholic, I assure you that you are. You wouldn't be thinking about it and you wouldn't be here if you weren't an alcoholic."[6] Using the disease analogy that AA itself uses for alcoholism, this is like saying that if you think a freckle is cancer then it is, because you wouldn't be thinking you had a disease unless you actually have one. Imagine the unnecessary terror and expense that would be generated if the medical profession applied the same reasoning as the self-help movement.

According to codependence leaders such as Bradshaw, Schaef, and Melody Beattie, everyone is sick until proven healthy. This rule particularly applies to anyone who works in a medical or mental health profession. "Co-dependents are servers," writes Schaef. "They are volunteers, the people who hold society to-gether, who set aside their own physical, emotional, and spir-itual needs for the sake of others."[7] While some would give these individuals awards for their service, Schaef seems to feel that they should undergo radical treatment for their desire to help others. In fact, she implies, the desire to help others is a signal of ineptitude: "Most mental health professionals are untreated co-dependents who are actively practicing their disease in their work in a way that helps neither them nor their clients."[8]

If codependence were a scientifically recognized disease, such a sweeping generalization would immediately be seized and dismissed by the scientific community, for it has no foundation either in fact or logic, but Schaef herself admits that codependence is no more than "a 'grass roots' idea. That is to say, people who admit to having the disease themselves . . . are developing theories about co-dependence, not professionals." In other words, this sickness that afflicts 100 percent—or more!—of us is not a disease but, at best, an idea and, at worst, a scam by the authors and therapists who have profited by treating, lecturing, and writing about it. Neither Schaef nor anyone else has conducted a survey of all mental health professionals to determine whether they suffer from this theoretical condition. And if Schaef's assessment of codependence is correct, the primary way helping professionals stop "practicing the disease" is to stop caring for others, which is hardly likely to improve the quality of mental health care for the client.

What does improve the quality of mental health care is a clear focus on health and normalcy as the ultimate objectives. When disease becomes the standard for normalcy, as it is for the co-dependence movement, the opportunity for complete recovery is eliminated and illness becomes a self-fulfilling prophecy. The names today's self-help groups choose to call themselves indicate just how far this reversal from health to disease has gone. The movement that began with Alcoholics Anonymous and led to Narcotics Anonymous has now brought us organizations such as Emotional Health Anonymous and Families Anonymous. Some of us take pride in our emotional health and our families, but apparently we should consider these to be shameful "diseases."

I am not suggesting that we should ignore real problems or try to wish them away, but neither should we undermine the resources that do exist in order to "treat" problems that don't. Unfortunately, that is often what happens in self-help groups. I first saw this process in action several years ago, after a shame, the method used to accomplish this is actually to intensify personal shame until it is absorbed into a collective shame that the entire group can share. The illusion is that by releasing your own shame to the group you are freed from it; in fact, the group cannot afford for you ever to free yourself of shame, for that would free you from the group. So even after thirty years of sobriety, even if he never takes another drink, the AA addict will continue to blame his alcoholism for his major failings and disappointments throughout the rest of his life. This is another of the great paradoxes of the Twelve Steps.

The overriding lesson of the Steps is not personal responsibility and morality, but conformity and dependence. In this regard, and in the insistence on a Higher Power in lieu of personal control, the Step programs parallel the temperance societies that flourished in the nineteenth century and ultimately pushed through Prohibition in 1920. The temperance movement, which maintained that the only way to control drinking is by abstaining completely, was patterned after Protestant revivalism. Individuals were expected to publicly admit their guilt and pledge their obedience to God in order to obtain group acceptance and absolution for their sins. Public confession, repentance, spiritual rebirth, and proselytization are all part of the Twelve Steps' fundamentalist religious underpinnings.

Of course, *the Twelve Steps were never intended for use by anyone except alcoholics.* After the steps were adopted by the nonalcoholic spouses of AA members, then by the children of alcoholics, they came to be viewed as a solution for anyone who was having difficulty coping with life. But this broad application of the program ignores the central role of abstinence in the program. Abstinence may be the best solution for addictions, say, to cigarettes or heroin, but do we really want God to strip us of all desire to eat, make love, or care for our friends and loved ones? The Twelve Steps demand all or nothing. All faith. All surrender. All abstinence. They do not encourage personal control or moderation, and they do not work for the majority of problems for which they're being used.

I do not agree with the Twelve Steps' fundamentalist assertion that we are all powerless before God. In fact, I would not even

friend of mine died of a stroke at age fifty, leaving his wife, Celia, a widow at forty-four. Theirs had been a close, supportive marriage. Celia had helped her husband, Mort, develop his business, and they'd had an active social life. When Mort died, his partners tried to buy Celia out of the business for a fraction of what she was due, and when she resisted they sued and she was forced to countersue. During her first months of widowhood, Celia was distraught over Mort's death and the vicious attacks from Mort's partners, whom she'd previously considered to be her friends. Acting on a neighbor's suggestion, she started going to a self-help group for widows.

At first, the group gave Celia the encouragement she needed to express her feelings and lean on others for consolation. But, unlike most mutual support groups for grieving spouses, this one had a leader who had been through codependence training. This, in fact, was her only training and, aside from her widowhood, her only qualification for leading the group. The women met in the basement of a church, but neither the church nor anyone else supervised the leader's performance. So, having been persuaded that her own emotional turmoil as a widow had been caused by her codependence, the leader had concluded that there is no such thing as a "normal" grieving process. Grief, she believed, was a symptom of disease. Unwilling to recognize the variability of human experience, she seemed determined to apply this narrow focus to everyone in the group, including Celia. After several weeks, she began to challenge Celia's comments about Mort and her legal difficulties. According to the leader, Celia's problems were caused not by Mort's death but by Celia's own disease. She had loved Mort too much. She was codependent—addicted to needing and being needed.

Fortunately, Celia had the sense to walk out of that group and never return. Within a few months, she had passed through the normal grieving process, was beginning to date, and had a new job, and the next year she won her legal battle. She cherished her memories of Mort and missed their life together, but she was also happy and active in her new independent life. Celia's emotional pain following her husband's death was no more a symptom of a disease than the physical pain accompanying a gunshot wound. Had she not had the confidence and common sense to reject her group leader's diagnosis, however, she might have spent the rest of her life in treatment for an imaginary addiction.

THE ALLURE OF THE VICTIM AND ADDICT LABELS

Forty years ago, Celia's reactions, both to her husband's death and to her group leader's accusations, would have been considered normal and justified. Today, they are exceptional. More and more people are *choosing* to be known as addicts or victims rather than competent, responsible individuals.

One reason is that these labels produce tangible benefits. When Dan White claimed that his addiction to junk food had impaired his judgment to such an extent that he didn't know how wrong it was to kill the mayor and supervisor of San Francisco, his "Twinkie defense" won him a reduced sentence. Hedda Nussbaum was absolved of guilt for the neglect and death of a child in her care because she had been a victim of spouse abuse. And Michael Deaver, former deputy chief of staff under President Ronald Reagan, received a suspended jail term after using alcoholism as his defense for perjuring himself during the Iran-Contra hearings. Addiction and victimization can buy clemency.

They can also buy media attention and remuneration. Ringo Starr made banner headlines for the first time in twenty years —and revived his career—by declaring himself a recovering drug addict. Betty Ford, Barbara Gordon, and Jill Robinson are just a few of the author-stars who have turned their past addictions into best-selling autobiographies, and even minor celebrities who would otherwise be ignored by the media now routinely barter their addictions into cover stories.

Victims, too, make sensational copy and are often showered with sympathy in the form of gifts and contributions. New York model Marla Hanson, whose face was slashed by attackers in 1986, received a donation of $20,000 to cover her medical bills.

The family of Jessica McClure, the child who was trapped in an abandoned well and rescued in front of TV cameras in 1987, also received substantial contributions that were placed in a trust fund for the girl. But such gifts often come with strings attached.

Victims and addicts are supposed to behave like victims and addicts, which means they can't get too healthy. After undergoing plastic surgery and resuming her career, Hanson was castigated by other models who were jealous of her success. "People only have so much sympathy," she discovered. "As soon as they think you are successful and you're doing well, they hate you."[9] McClure's parents were accused of misusing their daughter's trust fund for cars and jewelry—rumors that were never substantiated. Similar backlashes have plagued other victims, including a young boy in Tacoma, Washington, whose sexual attack and mutilation prompted his community to donate more than $600,000 and then reject his mother's plans for using the money. In short, victims who make suffering their career receive more encouragement than those who reject the victim role. Self-flagellation has not only become chic but is misconstrued as morality.

THE TWELVE STEP PARADOXES

Our cultural appetite for both a "kinder, gentler nation" and true confession mirrors the paradoxes of the Twelve Steps of Alcoholics Anonymous, which emphasize forgiveness and repentance while assigning the responsibility for recovery to a "Power Greater than Ourselves." I have done all these terrible things and hurt all these people, the program follower learns to say, and I am dreadfully sorry, but it wasn't really me doing it—it was this addiction, this disease over which I had no control. Now I still don't have any control over it, so I'm going to turn myself over to this Higher Power who will make everything all right, only it still won't be me doing it, so if it doesn't work it's not my fault. You can always blame the Higher Power.

Although the program is supposed to relieve individual

be discussing spirituality here if it did not figure so prominently in the self-help movement. But because millions of people are being trained to rely on faith to heal problems that they *have the power to resolve themselves*, I feel obligated to spell out my position. It is, essentially, existential. It is as follows:

No one is powerless. We all have certain strengths and limitations, some changeable and others permanent. And while we may not be able to control everything that happens to us, we *are* in charge of our responses, how we interpret and react to experiences. We have a vast array of choices regarding the way we conduct our lives, the people with whom we choose to associate, the values we decide to embrace. Everything we do reflects choices we have made, and, as a result, we are responsible for this behavior. This does not mean that we always understand our choices or make the right ones, but they are nevertheless our choices. When we make mistakes, we have the power to gather more and better information, so that we can correct or atone for the problem and make the right decisions in the future. This does not absolve us of responsibility for what we have done. Our errors are as much a part of us as our successes, but they are exactly that—a part. Our lives can be broken down into a great many parts, each of which can be labeled but none of which can label the whole person. This complexity, this endless array of possibilities, which not only informs our lives but characterizes our entire universe, is what I consider to be the essence of spiritual existence. Our moral responsibility is not "to turn our will and our lives over to the care of God," as the program's Step Three instructs, but to make the most constructive use of the opportunities that life has provided.

I agree with anthropologist Melvin Konner, who was so troubled by Boston Red Sox player Wade Boggs's public declaration of "sexual addiction" as the excuse for his philandering that he wrote: "We would all like to point at an illness—a psychiatric label—and say of our weak or bad actions, 'That thing, the illness, did it, not me. It.' But at some point we must draw ourselves up to our full height, and say in a clear voice what we have done and why it was wrong. And we must use the word 'I' not 'it' or 'illness.' I did it, I. *I*."[10]

THE ABUSE OF
THE VICTIM AND ADDICT LABELS

Self-identification and voluntary participation were the original cornerstones of the self-help movement. Group leaders were supposed to facilitate meetings but not issue advice. Participants were to identify their own needs and guide each other toward effective solutions based on personal experience. And public identification of members was expressly prohibited by the eleventh AA "Tradition," which states: "We need always maintain personal anonymity at the level of press, radio, or films." Ideally, each group would be nonprofessional, independent, anonymous, and democratic. According to AA founder Bill W., this would protect the organization and individual members against corruption by "those attitudes and practices which have sometimes demoralized other forms of human society."[11]

In theory these policies still define most of today's self-help groups, but in practice they are routinely violated. Since addiction is now chic, for example, anonymity is considerably less desirable than it was forty years ago and has effectively been dropped as a public relations requirement. For the truth is that anonymity would defeat the whole purpose for the many celebrities, authors, and self-appointed addiction experts who currently promote the Twelve Step programs. Name identification not only helps to attract new members to the movement but allows the spokespeople to boost their own reputations.

The original ban on professional involvement, too, is fading as more and more Step followers themselves become professional advocates of the program. Every one of the current self-help books on codependence was written by a "recovering codependent" who works the program and also makes a living by writing and advising others to follow the Steps. These advocates have a personal profit motive in bringing new blood into the movement, which is precisely what AA's founders intended to avoid by recommending a public relations policy based on "attraction rather than promotion."

Even though most self-help groups still advertise themselves as voluntary associations, the increased media attention given to addiction has greatly increased the social pressure for anyone even suspected of having a problem to get treatment. As a result, many of the people who end up in self-help groups are pushed into them by friends, family, employers, or, increasingly, by courts offering treatment as an alternative to jail for drunk drivers.

The line between voluntary and coerced participation has also been blurred by movement advocates who insist that anyone who refuses to admit his or her addiction is "in denial." Leaders of the codependence movement have institutionalized this practice by, on the one hand, proclaiming that our entire culture is codependent and, on the other, asserting that denial is one of the basic characteristics of codependence! In their analysis, healthy people do not exist, and claims of health are further proof of disease. The codependence gurus, in fact, do not want people to perceive themselves as normal, functioning adults but as defective children. "It's crucial to experience the powerlessness and unmanageability that results from being co-dependent," writes John Bradshaw. "*Fortunately*, millions are identifying themselves as codependents" [emphasis added].[12]

SELF-HELP "LEADERSHIP"

Anne Wilson Schaef echoes one of the recurrent themes of the self-help movement when she writes: "Objectivity is a myth. The people who can be trusted the most are those who can honestly say, 'I know how you feel because I have been there myself.' "[13] This theory explains why virtually every leader in the codependence movement is a self-described codependent, why the staunchest proponents of the disease theory of alcoholism have abused alcohol themselves, why the single most important criterion in selecting people to be leaders or sponsors in self-help groups is that they be addicts. However, while it may be true that people who have experienced your problems will know better what those problems feel like than others who have not, it is not true that their interpretations of those feelings will match yours. Take two women who have had abortions. One is relieved and thinks it was absolutely the right decision; the other is haunted by guilt because she feels that she has committed a mortal sin. These two women would probably not be very supportive or trusting of each other, even though they have been through the same experience. Nor would they be any better equipped to help resolve each other's problems. Most likely, they would simply try to win each other over to their respective—and diametrically opposed—positions.

If we accept that personal experience is the best gauge of insight, then we have to accept that only women are equipped to counsel women, only blacks to assist blacks, only Catholics to advise Catholics. But if your marriage was in trouble, would you prefer to take advice from someone who had a long, successful marriage or someone who was going through his fifth divorce? Although the divorcer would certainly identify with your crisis, would he be better equipped to help you *solve* your problem? The self-help philosophy might as well be that the best person to counsel a murderer is another killer, or that the person who really knows how to help you deal with your suicidal impulses is someone who is about to jump off a bridge. Understanding how a conflict feels does not automatically give you the tools to resolve it. The best counselor is not the one whose experience most closely resembles yours but the one who has been trained to understand both your problems and your feelings and who has the skills and knowledge to help you *solve* your problems.

Because the self-help movement is based on a nonprofessional, independent, and democratic model, it is not governed by any objective guidelines or supervisory agency. Anyone can start a self-help group. Anyone can run a Twelve Step program. And, unfortunately, many people have become leaders in the movement who really do not belong there.

My patient John is a case in point. Now twenty-four, he smoked marijuana for several years but quit on his own at age twenty-one. His younger sister, Betty, however, was a heroin addict who began to work the Twelve Step program after an overdose landed her in the hospital. Betty attended meetings once or twice a week and completely changed her lifestyle. She stopped seeing the friends with whom she had used drugs, concentrated on her schoolwork with an eye to attending law school, and gave numerous antidrug talks at local high schools. The Twelve Steps, she acknowledged, helped her to reshape her life, but after a year she was tired of being known as Betty the Addict. While she remained firmly committed to sobriety and the principles she had learned through AA, she felt that the group was like a treadmill that prevented her from closing the door on her past. She wanted to devote her energies to more constructive activities, so she stopped going to meetings.

This worried Betty's mother. The program had saved the girl's life. Despite Betty's unshakable commitment to sobriety, her mother was afraid that she might relapse after quitting the group. She also became convinced that her son needed to go through the program, too. John had been clean for three years but often got into trouble, took money from her without repaying it, lied to her about his whereabouts, and generally tried to manipulate her. According to the literature that Betty had shown her from group, this was the behavior of an addict. John might be "dry," but he was not "sober."

Then in his junior year of college and feeling overwhelmed by the academic and social pressures of school, John was more than willing to take refuge in a group where he could blame all his problems on an "addiction." Since he wasn't using drugs to begin with, he couldn't prove his rehabilitation with abstinence. Instead, he mastered the rhetoric. He was, he admitted, a dry drunk and an addict for life, but he was working a good program and getting honest with himself. His mother was proud of him, his sister supportive. His girlfriend, however, disagreed with both the rhetoric and its underlying assumptions.

Gina had started dating John several months before he joined the program and had watched its effect on his behavior and their relationship. Now, instead of worrying about his grades, he simply paid others to write his term papers and feed him final exam answers. He boasted about how he'd finally gotten smart and was not going to let the system get him down, and he seemed to have the same attitude toward Gina. No longer willing to listen to any opinions that differed from his own, he would harangue her with program rhetoric and badger her to attend meetings with him, even though she had never used drugs or alcohol. Apart from proselytizing, his only interest in the relationship seemed to be sexual. Finally, unable to reach him on her own, Gina threatened to break up unless he agreed to come with her for therapy.

In our first session, John used the Twelve Step jargon as a shield to deflect any question or comment that challenged his identity as a recovering addict. Gina, he said, could not possibly understand him until she admitted her own codependence. The proof that she was codependent, he argued, was her preoccupation with controlling him. As for himself, the proof of his sobriety was in his attendance record with the program. He was training to become a group leader and really felt that he was in tune with his process. He finally understood the power of non-rational, nonlinear thinking; he'd reached that hurt child inside and learned to surrender to pain. He'd gotten into his disease.

When I asked if Gina's report of his cheating was true, John said, "Yes, but so what? I'm honest with myself. I used to be a perfectionist, and it was paralyzing me. Now I realize that ninety percent of our educational system is a sham anyway. It's too hung up on useless analytic thinking. Even if the system calls it cheating, I know I'm doing what's best for me."

When I asked if he thought Gina's concern about the relationship was warranted, John replied, "The only thing that's wrong with our relationship is that Gina hasn't acknowledged her disease yet. She's just as addicted to her control trip as I am to drugs, and if she'd just get into a program she'd realize that our problems are really her problems."

But John was not being honest with Gina, his family, or himself. While his lack of self-awareness indicated a need for therapy, he did not belong in a Twelve Step program for drug addicts. Having joined the group, however, he not only began to view himself as an addict but to act like one, adopting the defensiveness and devious behavior patterns of other group members. The program had not cured his addictive behavior, it had induced it! At the same time, it had given him a rationale for his lifelong tendency to ignore his real problems and avoid responsibility.

The fact that no one in the group challenged John's identity as an addict or called his bluff when he began spouting program rhetoric, that he was actually considered a model for leadership, demonstrates a flaw common to many self-help groups. Often the only qualifications for becoming a group leader are membership in the group, familiarity with the program, and strong personal conviction. Emotional health and mental stability may even disqualify candidates because the leaders have to be able to identify with members who are in pain. But when leaders are *not* emotionally healthy, they can be a real threat to the others. I have seen self-help leaders verbally abuse and psychologically manipulate group members; they call it "confrontation" and claim that it's necessary to force the addict out of denial. In fact, the only real purpose of such tactics is to intimidate members into submission, but, once a leader is in place, there are few checks and balances to prevent abuses.

In my opinion, one of the most questionable practices of AA and groups patterned after it is the use of recovering addicts as sponsors. On the positive side, sponsors serve as surrogate best friends, available to meet or talk with their assigned charges at any time of the day and night, always willing to listen and empathize. And we all need friends, especially during times of crisis. But constructive friendships are based on mutual strengths, not weaknesses or addictions. They are voluntary, not assigned. And they assume relative equality rather than the kind of rescuer-rescuee relationship that occurs between sponsors and their charges. Sponsors assume the roles of friend, role model, and counselor but may be qualified for none of these. In fact, their sole qualification, in most cases, is being "in recovery." They are not required to have completed recovery (because these groups claim that no one is fully recovered), or to receive any special training, or even to have been sober for any specific length of time. Yet they are considered the lifeline for vulnerable individuals, often in emotional crisis, who depend on them for strength and guidance.

The use of addict sponsors is especially alarming when the charges are young people. Let me give you an example to show just how dangerous this system can be. One of my patients is a seventeen-year-old girl named Sandy who joined Overeaters Anonymous (OA) because she wanted to lose ten pounds.

Through the program she learned that her family and all her friends were responsible for the feelings of pain and rage that caused her to overeat. She learned that the only people she could really trust were the members of her group. She learned that the group was her "real" family, and that her sponsor was her best friend. Sandy's sponsor, Tina, was a forty-year-old woman who had been through AA and NA (Narcotics Anonymous) before joining OA. Tina had been an alcoholic for twenty years, a drug addict for ten, and had been clean and sober for less than one year when she became Sandy's sponsor. Tina had lost custody of her three young children when the court concluded that she was physically abusive to them, yet Sandy told me that she trusted Tina more than her own mother. After all, she said, Tina had done so much with her life; she had conquered all these addictions and was down to her last one. Tina was Sandy's role model. Thanks to Tina and OA, Sandy no longer had any friends her own age and was not speaking to her family.

Relationships that are based on mutual weakness cannot serve as sources of strength or enrichment. Unfortunately, self-help groups breed just this kind of connection. In the film *Beaches*, Bette Midler, playing a performer whose self-absorption nearly destroyed the most important relationships in her life, delivered a line that seems to me to capture perfectly the orientation of most self-help groups: "Enough about me," she says to her oldest friend. "How about you? What do you think about me?" Self-help groups cultivate self-involvement, often to the detriment of their members.

Elissa Schappell, a reporter who attended a series of meetings of Women Who Love Too Much (conducted according to guidelines offered in Robin Norwood's book of the same name), pointed out just how ineffective, and possibly even harmful, such groups can be:

> I see a lot of women here who have real problems they need to conquer. But the group seems to suppress any kind of emotion; instead, it offers up propaganda and a hollow spirit. The women seem to no longer think of themselves as Jane, a pianist, or Tess, a student, but as Jane, a Woman Who Loves Too Much, and Tess,

a Woman Who Loves Too Much. They wear the term "love addict" like a tag. And that is sad.

I don't know whether or not these women are truly love addicts. But I know that it's unlikely any of them could ever be remotely changed—not to mention cured—by the experience of being here. And yet they are addicted to this group, or to the idea of needing it; that much seems painfully clear. And that, I feel, is really Too Much.[14]

JUST HOW VOLUNTARY
IS SELF-HELP PARTICIPATION?

Which brings us back to the issue of voluntary participation. The AA Traditions state that the only requirement for membership in the program is a "desire to stop drinking" but, at the same time, that the organization's "common welfare should come first; personal recovery depends upon A.A. unity." What this means is that once you start working the program you are taught that your well-being, perhaps even your very survival, depends on the group. Following along with this reasoning, your participation is voluntary only to the extent that you are willing to risk your life by quitting the program. If you value your life, you will remain with the group, regardless of the quality of its leadership or your own specific needs. You will obey the Steps and keep coming back to the group because, according to the program, *you cannot rely on yourself.* •

This is not a minor point, and I do not believe that I am overstating it. There is a coercive undercurrent to the Twelve Step programs, and it is growing stronger as the movement gathers steam. It is especially apparent in the assertions and language of the codependence leadership:

• "Everyone has been violated emotionally. . . . Emotional violation is the most common core of our current cultural crisis."[15]

• "Take for granted that your situation is worse than you will allow yourself to acknowledge at present, and that your disease is progressing. Understand that you require appropriate treatment, that you cannot do it alone."[16]

• "Adult children *must* find a new family of affiliation. . . . The new family can be one of numerous 12-step groups. . . . A group is crucial because of the shame. The only way out of the shame is to embrace the shame."[17]

• "If you continue along your current path death and destruction await you. . . . But the moment you take that leap and say, 'Yes, I do have a problem. My love life is out of control. I can't do it myself. Please help me!' you will be free."[18]

• "If you believe you might be a candidate for any of the Twelve Step programs—if you even suspect you have a problem common to one of the groups . . . find a group and start going to meetings.[19]

These statements lead us to the inescapable conclusion that we are all very, very sick, and our only hope of survival is to spend the rest of our lives attending self-help meetings and working the Twelve Steps. Although offered in the name of help, they pressure us into doubting ourselves, our families, and society as a whole until the only institution we can trust is the Twelve Step program, and the only people we can trust are those who accept the Steps as their commandments. People, in other words, who admit that they are too sick or weak to function independently.

SELF-HELP:
AN EXERCISE IN "CODEPENDENCE"?

Ironically, the very traits that self-help leaders most frequently use to describe the "disease" of codependence describe the movement itself. This is not surprising, since the leaders all claim to be recovering codependents, but it has distressing implications for their followers. Let me explain by running through the top ten characteristics most commonly used to describe the codependent:

1. *Devoted to taking care of others.* If this is a sign of sickness, then the leaders of the movement are deathly ill, because they seem to be preoccupied with judging, instructing, and monitoring other people's lives. Hence, the flood of books, tapes, workshops, and self-help groups that spread the movement's message, virtually all created by recovering codependents committed to taking care of codependence in others.

2. *Feelings of low self-worth* are reflected in the leaders' insistence that only the diseased can recognize the disease, and also in the language of codependence, which uses an all-encompassing "we" to create statements such as: "Just keep doing the things we know we need to do. It will get better. Don't stop taking care of *us* no matter what happens."[20]

3. *Lying* is a strong term, but I believe the movement leaders are, in fact, lying to themselves and their followers when they proclaim their theories to be facts, when they make sweeping generalizations without substantiation, and when they insist that the Twelve Steps are the only—or even the best—treatment for all the conditions that they term addictions.

4. *Gullibility* is the fuel of deception. It enables the movement leaders to accept each other's theories and "findings" without challenging their basic assumptions or demanding proof, and it enables them to turn around and state their own theories as facts.

5. *Lack of respect for others* is a critical component of the movement's passion for branding *everyone* with a pathological label, regardless of actual symptoms or circumstances.

6. *Desire for control.* What better evidence of the leaders' desire to control than their insistence that every member of our society, indeed all of society itself, needs to read their books and accept their treatment.

7. *External referencing*, in codependence lingo, refers to a lack of personal boundaries, a need for validation from others. This underscores the movement leaders' passion for proselytizing and their satisfaction at the number of followers who agree to proclaim themselves diseased.

8. *Self-centeredness* is at the core of the movement's determination to impose its own narrow focus of psychology and human relationships on all of society.

9. *Fear, rigidity, and judgmentalism* are all elements of the movement's insistence on the Twelve Steps as the only path to salvation and its refusal to acknowledge the health or sanity of those who reject the Steps.

10. *Being out of touch with feelings.* People who are out of touch with their feelings are unable to communicate directly. They talk in circles and substitute abstract ideas for direct examples. The jargon of the codependence movement is a perfect example, with its use of "process" instead of emotion or thought, "working a good program" instead of living, "sobriety" instead of health and sanity.

Ultimately, if we are to resolve the specific problems that mark our lives we must move beyond stereotypes and labels and determine what it is that makes us unique, worthwhile, and strong. The answer to our private pain does not lie in universal theories but in the immediate reality of the choices we make every day. Learning to expand our options and make the right choices, to bring our problems into a realistic perspective, is what growth, sanity, and health are all about.

In these first chapters I have described how Twelve Step and codependence programs frequently misuse the disease model in treating problem behaviors and victims of abuse. I have presented some of the dangers of mistaking self-help organizations for religions and of using communities based on pathology as substitutes for family and friends. But knowing what's wrong with the self-help movement doesn't give you the *right* tools to help yourself. That's why I've written the second section of this book, which offers an eight-point plan to help you develop a positive, constructive approach to solving your problems and redefining your life. As you read through this next section, keep a pencil and paper handy. There will be exercises in each chapter to help you apply the recommended techniques directly to your own life.

NOTES

1. Beth Ann Krier, "Excess Baggage," *Los Angeles Times* (September 14, 1989): V20.

2. John Bradshaw, *Bradshaw on: The Family* (Deerfield Beach, Fla.: Health Communications, Inc., 1988), p. 166.

3. Anne Wilson Schaef, *When Society Becomes an Addict* (New York: Harper & Row, 1987), p. 15.

4. Benjamin Bloom, *Mastery Learning: Theory and Practice* (New York: Holt, Rinehart, and Winston, 1971), p. 19.

5. Lori and Bill Granger, *The Magic Feather: The Truth About Special Education* (New York: Dutton, 1986).

6. Stanton Peele, *The Diseasing of America* (Lexington, Mass.: Lexington Books, 1989), p. 89.

7. Schaef, p. 30.

8. Anne Wilson Schaef, *Co-Dependence: Misunderstood—Mistreated* (New York: Harper & Row, 1986), p. 4.

9. Ann Japenga, "Solace with Strings," *Los Angeles Times* (January 7, 1990): E1.

10. Melvin Konner, "The I of the Storm," *Los Angeles Times Magazine II* (October 8, 1989): 17.

11. Milton A. Maxwell, *The Alcoholics Anonymous Experience* (New York: McGraw Hill, 1984), p. 134.

12. Bradshaw, p. 180.

13. Schaef, *When Society Becomes an Addict*, p. 5.

14. Elissa Schappell, "In Rehab with the Love Junkies," *Mademoiselle* (October 1989): 253.

15. Bradshaw, pp. 144–45.

16. Robin Norwood, *Women Who Love Too Much* (New York: Pocket Books, 1986), p. 226.

17. Bradshaw, pp. 197–98.

18. Jed Diamond, *Looking for Love in All the Wrong Places* (New York: Avon Books, 1989), pp. 177–78.

19. Melody Beattie, *Codependent No More* (New York: Harper & Row, 1987), pp. 179–80.

20. Beattie, p. 214.

PART II

Completing Recovery:
An Eight-Point Plan

CHAPTER 4

Define Your Problems Without Labeling Yourself

One reason for the great popularity of the self-help movement is that it provides a vast array of problem labels from which to pick and choose. Do you hurt because you're a woman who loves too much? Are you out of control because you're an addict, victim, or adult child? Or is your life a mess because you're codependent? You can pick a label for yourself and interpret your problems to conform to it. But that does nothing to alleviate your pain, and it adds the extra burden of a painful identity: from a person with problems you become a problem person.

Here are two vignettes that illustrate just how easy it is to slip into a "problem person" category:

• A letter to Ann Landers refers to a prior letter from a woman who confessed that she used her "fortress of fat" to avoid intimacy with other people. The second writer identifies herself as an Adult Child of an Alcoholic and beseeches the original writer to do as she did and join an ACA group—even though there is no indication that the "fat" woman came from an alcoholic family![1]

• I was consulted by the family of an elderly woman who had

shot her husband in the head. The woman was suffering from Alzheimer's disease, and her husband had threatened to institutionalize her. This was her second marriage, and although her first husband had been an alcoholic, this one was not. When I asked her daughter (a member of Adult Children of Alcoholics) why her mother had killed her husband, the daughter responded, "She's codependent," as if that explained everything.

In her book *Co-Dependence*, Anne Wilson Schaef implies that all women are codependent merely by virtue of their gender: "Since many co-dependents are women, and since many women are thought to be co-dependent, women's issues are intimately related to co-dependence."[2] Using the disease analogy so often touted by the codependence movement, this is like saying that, since many cancer patients are women and many women have cancer, cancer is intimately related to women's issues. Or that sickle cell anemia is intimately related to black issues. Since many children are blond and many blonds are children, does this make blondness a childhood issue? The reasoning is so ludicrous that it should be dismissed without further consideration, except that it reflects the thinking that runs throughout the self-help movement and illustrates why it is so important for *you* to scrutinize your own problems and assess them for what they are rather than try to fit them into someone else's formula.

You may have made poor choices. You may have had traumatic experiences. You may have some bad habits or unmet needs. You may be operating on misinformation. Or maybe you simply don't have the resources you need to improve your life. These are all real problems, but they do not constitute the sum total of your life. They are not your identity. And having problems does not mean that *you* are a problem.

ISSUES VS. PROBLEMS

Another common mistake is to confuse issues with problems. Instead of identifying what's not working in our lives in simple, concrete terms, the pseudopsychology of the self-help movement has created a litany of issues to globalize our pain. Instead of learning how to cut back on our eating or drinking or how to combat depression and loneliness, we are told that the recovery process must confront our inner shame, our lack of boundaries, our delusion and denial, our hidden dependency, and the hurt child within us. Even the terms "addiction" and "victimization," which formerly were used to describe specific problems, have been transformed by the self-help movement into issues so general that their meaning has become hopelessly muddled.

I see this shift from problems to issues in the advice doled out in magazine articles, in the language used in recovery groups and workshops, and especially in the assumptions that patients bring with them when they enter therapy. I will ask a couple to describe the problems they are having in their marriage and the wife will say that her husband is insensitive; he is controlling; he doesn't know how to be an equal partner because he's a child of an alcoholic. The husband will say that his wife is hypercritical; she doesn't respect his unmet needs; when he lost his job three years ago, she wasn't there for him. They are surprised and confused when I tell them they are describing issues, not problems. So I ask them to stop analyzing what's going on and just describe the events that are causing conflict in their marriage *now*. Only then do I discover that no one in the family has shopped for groceries in over a month because they cannot agree about whose job it should be. *That* is a tangible problem. By focusing on that problem and working together to resolve it, we can begin to deal with many of the issues that surround it. It is much more difficult (and often impossible) to start with issues and work inward toward the problems.

Ironically, while our lives are filled with discrete, highly specific events and details, most of us prefer to describe our experiences and feelings as issues. There is a natural tendency to sum things up, to interpret and analyze our experiences so that they fit into some logical pattern. This interpretive process, however, can accomplish two additional, less obvious, and often destructive, functions. It may rearrange actual events to fit a socially acceptable or desirable theory. And it seals those original details in a framework that may be extremely difficult to change.

The fact that your husband serves you frosted cereal when he knows that you're dieting thus is transformed into proof that he is sabotaging your effort to lose weight (as your Overeaters Anonymous group has warned you he might) and precipitates an argument that leaves you both depressed and angry because it escalates a relatively minor incident into a major marital confrontation in which neither you nor your husband are willing to admit defeat.

IDENTIFYING ISSUES

Issues often deal with the history, or assumed history, of a problem. They are the background information that we use to explain (often inaccurately) why other people hurt us. And in many self-help groups they are the primary focus of attention and the source of the "problem person" label the group assigns to its members. Let me give you an example. Two weeks after her thirty-ninth birthday, Janine decided that her self-help group was not working for her and she needed professional help. This is how she described herself, her voice flat and dejected, in our first session together.

> I'm an adult child of an alcoholic. My dad was the drinker, and my mother put up with that. She had two jobs, plus taking care of me and my sister. But when my father had an affair she couldn't handle it. When I was twelve, they got a divorce and she went to pieces. I was the one who took care of her—my sister was younger and never considered it her responsibility. I never forgave my father, but I guess I still loved him because when he died this year I got so depressed, and I just can't snap out of it. I joined an Adult Children of Alcoholics group to see if they could help me, but I'm not convinced that it accomplishes all that much to keep dwelling on my relationship with my dad. I

mean, he's dead now. And nothing I can say is going
to bring him back or change the relationship we had.

When I asked Janine to list her problems individually, every
item on her list was either historical (dealing with past experiences or emotions) or interpretive (assumption or analysis of
why an event occurred or what is motivating someone else). In
fact, these were not problems at all, but issues:

- I don't think my father ever really loved me.
- Because I grew up in an alcoholic family, I never learned
  to separate my needs from those of the people around me.
- As a child, I was ashamed of my family.
- I have always had to shoulder more than my share of responsibility for my mother and the family because my sister
  is so self-absorbed.

Janine's ACA group had trained her to view these issues as
problems, but problems are much narrower in scope and can
be defined in concrete terms. They are immediate, and they
affect how we feel and behave *today*, not how we felt three years
ago or how we will feel next year. They involve conflicts that
can be resolved, not lost causes or impossible dreams. And they
are "I-oriented," that is, they belong to us and cannot be assigned or blamed on anyone else. Whether or not Janine's sister
was self-absorbed was not Janine's problem; Janine's own *current* feelings toward her sister, however, might be.

The only concrete problem Janine was able to identify in that
first session was her depression. It was depression that had
prompted her to join ACA in the first place, and it was the
group's failure to relieve her depression that had persuaded her
to try therapy. Had she not been depressed and unhappy, she
would simply have accepted her past experiences for what they
were: part of her life. She might have thought about her childhood and her family's behavior and arrived at an interpretation
of her own responses, but these analyses would not still be
dominating her thoughts at age thirty-nine had she been satisfied
with her work and home life. In short, if it weren't for her
problems, Janine's issues would seem insignificant.

IDENTIFYING GENERAL PROBLEMS

Janine's ACA group had told her that her unhappiness was caused by her relationship with her father and by his alcoholism. But when we examined other aspects of her life, she began to see that her unhappiness might stem from different and unrelated problems. She had recently moved across country at her sister's suggestion, but almost as soon as she arrived her sister was transferred. Janine decided to stay on, even though she had no friends and was so shy that she did not make new friends easily. She worked as a copywriter for a small advertising agency, and, although she enjoyed her work, she resented having to deal with the firm's internal politics. Janine had a history of clinical depression, for which she had been on medication for nearly two years during college. And finally, though she was reluctant to discuss this, she worried that she would never get married and that she might already be too old to have children. Janine's sister, whom she referred to as a "supermom," was married and had a new baby, as well as a successful law career. Janine had always planned to have a family but complained that she was only attracted to "jerks," never to nice men who were interested in marriage or even treated her decently. In fact, ever since her father died, she'd been terrified that she was destined to grow old alone.

Suddenly, we had a broad assortment of problems to deal with. These were not shadows from the distant past or motives that Janine had pinned on someone else. They were troubled feelings and tangible conflicts that she was experiencing in her present life. Our next task was to sort them out, to put them into an organized framework so that we could begin to understand and resolve them.

We started by reviewing the criteria for defining problems. Problems are feelings, beliefs, or activities that:

- Are narrow in scope
- Can be defined in concrete terms
- Exist now, not three years ago or next year

- Involve conflicts that can be resolved, not lost causes or impossible dreams
- Are "I-oriented"—cannot be assigned to or blamed on anyone else

When Janine was clear about the difference between issues and problems, she began to isolate her general problems, starting with her feelings and beliefs:

- I feel depressed all the time.
- I'm lonely.
- I'm not happy with my job.
- I'm jealous of my sister.
- I feel unloved.
- I think I'm going to miss out on something vital if I don't have a child.
- I'm starting to think of myself as an old maid—a spinster.

Then she described in general terms the difficulties she was having functioning:

- I'm not doing very good work.
- I always choose the wrong kind of men.
- I don't know how to deal with office politics.
- I don't know how to make new friends in this town.

Now we had identified eleven general problems that were contributing to Janine's unhappiness. But how serious were these problems, really? Janine was too close to them to know. She needed some objective standards to gauge their severity.

WHAT IS A SERIOUS PROBLEM?

It is a truism that the person you know best is the person you know least: yourself. And the problems that seem overwhelming to you today may seem relatively insignificant when viewed through someone else's eyes, or even through your own eyes five years from now. At the same time, you may overlook or exaggerate problems because of mistaken assumptions about what's normal. For example, if everyone you know has stopped drinking, you may worry that you are an alcoholic because you occasionally have a glass or two of wine, even though you never drink to intoxication. Alternatively, if you and your friends routinely drink six or seven beers apiece, you may view this as perfectly normal behavior even though you've been arrested several times for drunk driving.

It is impossible to tell how serious your problems really are without stepping back, getting a new perspective, and considering the effect of these problems on your life. Only then can you tell which deserve your immediate attention, which can be resolved over time, and which are not problems at all.

It's not easy to step back from your problems when you are consumed with unhappiness. If it were, there would be far less demand for psychotherapy. However, if you listen to the feedback that your family and friends are giving you, if you stop focusing on symptomatic behavior and look instead at the physical evidence of your lifestyle and the *consequences* of your actions, you can probably collect enough objective information to measure your problems against the following criteria:

A serious problem can be harmful to your physical and mental health. For most people, smoking would not be a problem if it did not increase the risk of cancer and early death. Statistically this increased risk is a fact. Yet there are people who refuse to consider their smoking a problem, and some of them will get away with smoking to a ripe old age. While it's important to recognize potentially harmful attitudes and behaviors, it's also important to realize that almost everything we do involves hazards. Eating fruit and meat, jogging, driving, and making love are all potentially life-threatening. So, we've been told, is codependence. So is breathing. Whether we choose to identify these behaviors as *serious problems* has a lot to do with their relative costs and benefits and our information sources. We all routinely make trade-offs—living in polluted areas because the work we love or need keeps us there; staying married even though we argue, because most other aspects of the relationship are satisfying; caring for our children despite their endless demands because we are responsible for them and because we love them. Ultimately we must rely on common sense to decide how a given situation or course of action will affect us. If it is doing us more good than harm, we're not likely to consider it a serious problem.

A serious problem may make it difficult to lead a normal life. One of the distinctions between moderate drinkers and alcoholics is that moderate drinkers can hold a job, sustain a marriage, and maintain a normal range of activities despite their drinking. Alcoholics very often can't. A similar line divides those of us with ordinary phobias, such as a general discomfort in high or enclosed spaces, from true agoraphobics, who are so terrified of being out in public that they cannot leave the house. The more a problem interferes with our ability to function, the more severe that problem is.

A serious problem can cause feelings of guilt and shame. These feelings reflect an assumption that our behavior is abnormal and wrong. A woman who has been raped may feel as guilty and shameful about "allowing" herself to be victimized as a man who hits his wife every time he loses his temper. The two situations both represent serious problems; however, the rape victim's primary conflict involves her beliefs about the attack (e.g., that she was somehow responsible or provoked the rape), while the batterer's main problem is his actual behavior. Guilt and shame are often signals, offshoots of problems or secondary problems, but they should not be confused with the primary problem itself.

A serious problem may attract negative comments or criticism from others. If a woman's husband says that their insurance rates have gone up because she's gained so much weight, and her mother gives her a diet book for her birthday, and she overhears her children's friends making fat jokes about her, she has to realize that her weight is a serious problem. When other people notice that our behavior or attitudes or feelings are unhealthy or dangerous, we may feel like blaming the messenger, but we probably will do better to heed the message. The same applies when we try to hide our behavior because we know that others will consider it abnormal. The bulimic who covers the sound of her vomiting by flushing the toilet may fool her family, but she knows that her behavior is not normal or healthy, and concealing it won't make it so. Consistently negative feedback from people whose judgment we respect is a clear signal that we have a serious problem.

A serious problem can lead to illegal or immoral conduct. When our lives are dominated by a serious problem our judgment may falter, we may become so desperate for even temporary relief that we are willing to act in ways that we know are wrong. One of the many reasons that poverty, drug addiction, illiteracy, and unemployment are serious problems is that they frequently push those afflicted into illegal and immoral activities. Likewise, when depression, jealousy, and anger become intense or chronic conditions, they can lead to suicide, physical violence, or emotional cruelty. That risk is what ultimately defines their severity. In fact, the mere temptation to engage in illicit conduct can signal a serious problem.

PRIORITIZING GENERAL PROBLEMS

After going through this list of criteria, Janine was able to identify which of her problems were serious. Her depression and loneliness, her difficulties at work and with men, and her conflicted feelings about her sister, having a child, and getting older all needed to be resolved. But in Janine's mind, these problems were woven so tightly together that she couldn't prioritize them.

She didn't know which to tackle first, which was the most pressing.

To help Janine prioritize her problems, I asked her the following questions:

- Is any of your problems an immediate threat to your health or life?
- What is causing you the most discomfort now?
- What do you think will cause you the most discomfort a year from now?
- What consumes most of your thoughts?
- What causes you the most anxiety?
- What do you most frequently dream about?
- What causes the most disruption in your life?
- Which of your problems demands your immediate attention and/or decision?

These questions all dealt with three basic considerations that determine the relative urgency of problems: The first consideration is endangerment. A problem that poses an imminent threat to one's own or someone else's life must always take top priority. A problem that is a long-term threat is less urgent because it may resolve itself as the surrounding problems are solved, but it still deserves close attention. Janine didn't see any of her problems as an immediate threat, but she thought she might be capable of suicide if she didn't get some relief from her depression.

The second consideration is discomfort. Although Janine originally thought her most serious problems had to do with her family relationships, she realized through this line of questioning that she spent most of her time wrestling with the deadening sensation of depression. Of all her problems, this clearly was causing her the most discomfort and disruption. The problems that occupied most of her thoughts and made her the most anxious, however, were her social difficulties—her inability to make friends or sustain a fulfilling sexual relationship.

The third consideration in prioritizing problems is the need for an immediate decision. If a decision must be made within a few days or weeks, then making that decision may be the most urgent problem even if it causes the least discomfort. Often, in fact, we exaggerate the severity of other problems simply to avoid making important decisions. Although Janine did not spend a great deal of time thinking about whether or not she would have a child, and this question caused her far less anxiety than her lack of a satisfying sexual relationship, her age gave it a special urgency. If she made up her mind to have a child she could still do it as a single mother, but she needed to decide soon, one way or another. Likewise, her job dissatisfaction seemed to Janine to be less important than her depression and social woes, but if she didn't begin to deal with it soon, she was likely to be unemployed.

After reviewing these considerations, Janine was able to rank her problems from most to least urgent:

1. Depression
2. Poor job performance
3. Loneliness/Inability to make friends
4. Desire to have a child
5. Lack of success with men
6. Envy of sister's achievements
7. Negative attitude about aging

But these were still very broad descriptions. We needed to see how Janine's general problems translated into everyday life. We needed to refine them into specific problems.

IDENTIFYING SPECIFIC PROBLEMS

Specific problems are like spokes radiating from the hub of a wheel. The general problem is the hub, and the source, of the specific conflicts, which may extend into several different aspects of life. All the same criteria that apply to general problems apply to the specifics, only more so. They are narrower, more concrete, more immediate, easier to resolve, and more "I-oriented." Thus, while the couple I mentioned earlier in this chapter had a general problem with communication, one of their specific problems was to work out a plan for the grocery shopping.

The best way to identify specific conflicts is to look at how each general problem translates into the three basic areas of experience: emotions, behavior, and attitude or beliefs. Take, for example, Janine's depression. I asked her to describe precise situations in which her depression affected her emotionally. "When I wake up in the morning," she answered, "I feel blank, numb, like there's a dead weight holding me down." Her emotional reactions to other people were also affected: "At work someone will tell me a story or a joke, and I feel like I can't connect with what they're saying. Nothing seems funny to me anymore or even interests me." Janine's lethargy and lack of motivation, particularly in the morning, and her inability to connect emotionally to other people were two specific emotional problems caused by her depression.

I asked her to describe comparable situations in which her depression was disrupting her behavior or activities. For openers, she said, she slept an average of eleven hours a day. After getting home from work she would often cry uncontrollably for as long as a half-hour. She had little appetite and had lost about ten pounds over the past six months. She was frequently late to work and sometimes didn't make it in at all. She had trouble concentrating and, as a result, felt that the quality of her work was so poor that she might be fired. Each of these was a separate behavioral problem that demanded attention.

Finally, we looked at the ways in which Janine's depression was affecting her attitudes and beliefs. She wasn't sure what I meant by this, so I asked what she thought of herself. "I think I'm pretty useless," she replied. I asked what she expected to happen to her in the future. "I don't think I really have a future. I guess I've been so flattened emotionally that I just can't see beyond the next twenty minutes." Janine's low self-worth, her nihilistic view of the future, and her preoccupation with her immediate situation were specific attitudinal problems, all stemming from her depression.

Even if you cannot reform whole patterns of behavior overnight, by dividing your problems into manageable increments you can begin to make some progress, and that progress, however minor, will motivate you to keep going. When Janine began therapy she was overwhelmed by issues that she could not change and problems that were too enmeshed to see clearly. She was staring into a jungle that seemed impenetrable. But by first weeding out the ancient and irresolvable issues and then winnowing her problems into small, focused segments, she gradually acquired a different perspective. As bleak as she still felt, she was beginning to face her troubles with the hope that she would be able to move past them.

IDENTIFY YOUR ISSUES AND PROBLEMS

Now it's your turn to identify your issues and problems.

1. Start by listing the five issues that cause you the most concern. (Five is a manageable number, but the length of the list is not really important as long as you identify all the key issues that are causing you distress.) Remember, issues are often shaped by our interpretations of other people's attitudes toward us. They tend to be general, historical, and causal in nature, and are often impossible to resolve completely. They may include past problems with family members or friends, your analysis of recent conflicts, or experiences that bother you to the point of affecting your behavior but which you cannot control.

Examples of issues:

- My father always favored my sister when we were growing up.
- My grandparents were alcoholics.
- My brother was killed in a car accident when I was ten.
- I was fondled by the next-door neighbor when I was three.
- My husband never really wanted to marry me.

The five **issues** that cause me the most concern are:

1. _____
2. _____
3. _____
4. _____
5. _____

2. Next, list the general problem areas that cause the most conflict in your life right now. These include feelings, beliefs, and behaviors that:

- Are narrow in scope
- Can be defined in concrete terms
- Exist *now*, not three years ago or next year
- Involve conflicts that *can* be resolved, not lost causes or impossible dreams
- Are "I-oriented"—cannot be assigned or blamed on anyone else, and are within your power to control—even if you do not *feel* that you are in control of them right now.

Examples of general problem areas:

- My husband and I hardly ever talk to each other anymore.
- I need to lose twenty pounds.
- I'm so afraid of crime that I can't leave my house.
- I can't sustain a committed relationship for more than three months.

If you have difficulty identifying your problems, the following suggestions may help you develop a clearer, more accurate perspective:

- Stop trying to fit yourself into the mold of a sick person or victim and focus on the individual circumstances of your current life.

• Brainstorm all your problems, not just the most obvious or troublesome ones. Make lists, and include even the most irrational or embarrassing problems, even conflicts that you don't believe are serious problems but that bother you nevertheless.

• Look at yourself both subjectively (through your own eyes) and objectively (through other people's eyes). Talk to your family, friends, and co-workers, and try to establish how they view you, what they observe as your most significant problems. Particularly if you have a problem behavior, such as drinking, gambling, or using drugs, others may see it as a problem before you do, but if you look at yourself through their eyes, you may see it, too.

• Don't try to analyze or figure out why you have a particular problem, just concentrate on how it affects you.

General problem areas that are causing the most conflict in my life right now are:

1. _____

2. _____

3. _____

4. _____

5. _____

3. Now evaluate the severity of these problems by indicating on the chart on page 81 the statements that are *true* for each item on your list. If true, write in the space provided the "score" that follows that statement (the number in parentheses).

GENERAL PROBLEM

1	2	3	4	5

This is more of a problem for me than it is for most other people. (2)

This problem is harmful to my health. (3)

This problem poses a threat to my life. (4)

This problem makes me feel guilty and shameful. (1)

Other people have noticed and commented that this is a problem for me. (2)

This problem is making it difficult for me to lead a normal life. (3)

I would be far happier if I could resolve this problem. (1)

Because of this problem, I have engaged in illegal or immoral conduct. (3)

I am willing to take whatever steps are necessary to put this problem behind me. (2)

TOTAL (add down for each column)

Now total your scores for all true statements under each problem. To evaluate the severity of each problem, locate your total scores on the chart below.

Score	Evaluation
12–21	Moderately severe to very severe problem: requires immediate attention and possibly professional intervention.
8–12	Moderate problem: requires attention to prevent it from worsening.
0–8	Not a significant problem: stay alert to make sure that it does not worsen, but you can probably keep it under control without outside assistance.

4. Finally, break down the general problems on which you scored between 8 and 21 into related specific conflicts. Do this by identifying highly concrete ways in which each general problem translates into the three experiential areas: emotion, behavior, and attitude or belief.

Example:

General problem: I am forty pounds overweight.

Specific emotional problem: I'm ashamed to be seen in a bathing suit or nude, even by my husband.

Specific behavioral problem: I get winded and exhausted easily whenever I work out, which keeps me from exercising as much as I should.

Specific attitudinal problem: I think that I'm a source of embarrassment for my husband, even though he claims to love me.

Example:

General problem: I worry about my husband's drinking.

Specific emotional problem: I dread his return at the end of each day for fear he will come home drunk.

Specific behavioral problem: I waste hours every day checking around the house for hidden bottles and calling his office to make sure he's where he's supposed to be.

Specific attitudinal problem: I think I'm somehow responsible, that I've enabled him to develop a drinking problem.

Specific **emotional, behavioral**, and **attitudinal conflicts** that have resulted from my general problems are:

GENERAL PROBLEM: _____

Specific emotional problem: _____

_____

Specific behavioral problem: _____

_____

Specific attitudinal problem: _____

_____

GENERAL PROBLEM: _____

Specific emotional problem: _____

_____

Specific behavioral problem: _____

_____

Specific attitudinal problem: _____

_____

GENERAL PROBLEM: _____

Specific emotional problem: _____

_____

Specific behavioral problem: _____

_____

Specific attitudinal problem: _____

_____

Now you have a clear idea of your issues and how they differ from your problems. You have an assessment of the relative severity of your problems. And you can see how your general problems break down into specific conflicts. The next step is to investigate how your problems evolved.

NOTES

1. Ann Landers, "Burden of Children of Alcoholics," *Los Angeles Times* (August 16, 1989): V9.

2. Anne Wilson Schaef, *Co-Dependence: Misunderstood—Mistreated* (New York: Harper & Row, 1986), p. 11.

CHAPTER 5

Recognize the Many Different Influences That Have Shaped Your Life

We all have a tendency to hide behind labels rather than confront our own contradictions. How can one person possibly be an unfaithful spouse but also a loving parent, a neglected child but a happy adult, an unethical professional but a responsible citizen, all at the same time? Each identity seems to rule out the others. Instead of trying to explain or resolve the contradictions, most people who fit such an untidy profile adopt one, maybe two of the labels as a public persona and conceal the rest. This deceit may produce a superficially neat exterior, but it does nothing to alleviate the confusion within.

Recovery is like a reconstruction project. Before you remodel your home, you need to assess the surrounding neighborhood, the strengths and weaknesses of the basic structure, the materials you have to work with. Otherwise, you may add a second story, paper over the walls, and lay on new paint without ever realizing that the building sits on a major fault line or, alternatively, that it has a marvelous old brick facade buried beneath the plaster. You'll overlook serious liabilities and unexpected assets. So, too, as you work toward recovery, you need to recognize both the positive and negative influences that have shaped your life.

THE FAMILY FACTOR

The codependence movement insists that our gravest problems as individuals and as a society stem from our dysfunctional families. And not necessarily the families of our adolescence or remembered childhood. According to John Bradshaw, many of our problems are rooted in babyhood: "Unresolved infancy needs are like a hole in your psyche—they manifest as a craving, a kind of insatiable void."[1] This psychic hole turns us into "lost children" who try too hard to do well, who have trouble socializing, who feel vaguely depressed, who are addicted to something—anything.

It is convenient and wonderfully simple to pin all our troubles on our parents. It's all their fault, we tell ourselves, so there's nothing much we can do about it but learn to love ourselves and surround ourselves with others who love us exactly as we are. And the codependency movement is thoughtfully providing thousands of groups where we're assured of finding this sort of blind acceptance. Easy answers, easy solutions, except that life is not that simple.

I do not deny that dysfunctional families exist. Drug and alcohol addiction, physical and sexual abuse, and emotional instability in the home can have severe effects on children. But as Emmy Werner's research (see chapter 1) shows, for every child who suffers lasting scars, there are others who are able to function well and are content with their lives. Yet I see patients who have been persuaded by the codependence movement that, because they were raised in an abusive or alcoholic family, they must be in denial if they think that they're okay.

Even more disturbing to me as a psychologist is the self-help movement's tendency to label virtually every family as dysfunctional and then apply the same brand of denial to anyone who claims emotional stability. These feelings of imposed co-dependence are reflected in an article by one of the participants in a four-day workshop for "recovering family members" in Houston, Texas. The article's author, Skip Hollandsworth, reports that Bradshaw and other leaders of the workshop informed participants that the signals of "covert dysfunction" in families include spankings, parental nudity, and too much parental praise for children's accomplishments! Hollandsworth writes:

> I assumed I had grown up in one of those rare func-tional families—a household that despite normal amounts of arguing and the usual lack of communica-tion, was filled with love and encouragement to find one's own way in life. But . . . by the third day of the workshop, I was giving in. I was reevaluating those periodic feelings of loneliness and ambiguity I had ex-perienced throughout my life, those moments when I had felt little self-worth. I started asking if it was not all part of some larger pattern of codependency. Maybe I hadn't received enough affection; maybe my parents had spent too much time telling me I "should" or "ought to" do things; maybe I had been taught early on to lie in order to fit into the highly polished family image; maybe I had tried too hard to please everyone else.[2]

By the end of the workshop, Hollandsworth reports, nearly all of the seven people in his group announced plans to seek therapy and join some sort of Twelve Step program. One was contem-plating divorce as a result of the workshop, and another was going to postpone her pending marriage. It was as if this "co-dependence training" had stripped away all their individual cop-ing mechanisms and healthy defenses, and reduced them to a common perspective. They had become fearful, intense, and unable to trust their own instincts.

As Hollandsworth's report illustrates, we are each the pro-duct—the constantly *changing* product—of a vast array of in-fluences. Family certainly is an important variable, but so are experiences like this workshop. So are school and the people in our neighborhoods. So are biological factors, such as temperament, health, and nutrition. So are the cultural and political conditions of our time. And so are critical life experiences, such as getting hired and fired, marrying and raising children, losing a loved one, or being victimized by violent crime.

Some of these variables are random and unrelated, while others do connect. But the connections are often circuitous and tenuous. You may have been mugged because you live in a dangerous neighborhood because you can't afford to move because you lost your job because you never finished school because you had to take care of your family because your parents were alcoholics and never gave you the love or support you needed. This does not mean that you were mugged because your parents never loved you. It means that your parents were part of a complex of circumstances that increased your risk of ultimately being victimized. Blaming your current problems entirely on your family is far more likely to prevent you from solving these problems than to help you deal with them effectively.

Among the patients I have "inherited" from the codependence movement is a woman in her late thirties named Jane. Three years before I first met her, Jane started having problems in her job as a bank vice president. She'd been bypassed for several promotions and didn't feel she was assertive or competitive enough. Her failure disturbed her because she was extremely bright and capable, and her parents and husband had always encouraged her to pursue a high-powered career. So she sought help from a counselor whose specialty happened to be codependence. Soon he had convinced her that her problems could be traced to the fact that her parents, who shared one or two ritual cocktails every evening, were alcoholics. He urged her to join ACA, which she did, and he guided her through numerous encounter-style exercises designed to help her "get her anger out." After listening to Jane describe her childhood, the counselor concluded that her parents had emotionally abused her by lying to her. They'd told her she was pretty when, by her own admission, she was a very homely child. They told her she was brilliant when she was really just average in intelligence. They told her she could be anything she wanted to be even though they really wanted her to be a superachiever. And, of course, they made her think that they had no problems of their own when, in fact, they were alcoholics.

"I deluded myself for thirty-five years in thinking that I loved them," Jane explained, "but I really had all this unexpressed rage toward them. I just needed therapy and ACA to help me learn how to feel it."

Not only had Jane learned to express her anger toward her parents, whom she had unilaterally shut out of her life, but she accused her husband of "ambushing" her the same way her father had with sarcastic and manipulative comments, bribery, and underhanded compliments. Her husband told her he loved her, and she said he was lying. He gave her presents, and she said he was trying to buy her off. He attempted to make love to her, and she said he was sexually abusive. Finally, when she stopped sleeping with him altogether, he insisted that she consult a different therapist. Their family doctor recommended me.

Jane's family background sounded suspiciously normal, but rather than contradict in our first session what her counselor had spent two years teaching her, I began asking questions about her school experiences. Did she enjoy school? Was she good at sports? Was there much social pressure at her school? Had she had close friends? Did she have any teachers that made a particular impression on her? When she got older, did boys ask her out on dates? Did she get into the college of her choice?

At first, Jane was reluctant to explore this school business. "What's that got to do with anything?" she demanded.

"Well," I replied, "you spent more time during your first eighteen years at school or with school friends than you did with your family. So it probably had at least as significant an impact on your emotional health during that period as anything your parents said or did to you."

That was an understatement. Jane had been tall, gawky, and pale as a child, and from her first day of kindergarten the other children teased her relentlessly. They nicknamed her Stretch and ridiculed her lack of coordination. She was always the last to be picked for teams. She had no close friends, was never part of any cliques, and when she sought protection from her teachers she was tagged a teacher's pet. By the time Jane reached junior high school she was a full head taller than the tallest boy in her class, and there was no turning back from her role as a social misfit. She hunched her shoulders and wore drab clothes so as not to call attention to herself and was unable to look her class-mates, especially boys, in the eye. She became an academic superachiever not to please her parents but because it distracted her from the social rejection she experienced in school. Although she came out of her shell in college and discovered that she was actually quite good-looking, she felt the same old waves of panic and shame wash over her when she attended her twentieth high school reunion.

Perhaps Jane's parents could have taken less pride in their daughter, been more honest in their appraisal of her, more aware of what she was going through at school. But Jane's problems as a child appeared to have far more to do with her peers than her parents. And it seemed likely that her problems with as-sertiveness and competition at work had more to do with con-ditioning she'd received in school than any dysfunction at home. It also seemed that the conditioning she'd received as an "ACA" might have done irreparable damage to her marriage and to her relationship with her parents, not to mention her career, where her new angry-woman act had so offended her boss (another woman) that she'd been demoted. She was going to have to find a way to get rid of some of that anger she had so carefully cultivated, or her problems were likely to get a whole lot worse before they got better.

IT'S YOUR NATURE

One of psychology's oldest questions is whether our personalities are preprogrammed by nature or whether they reflect the qual-ity of nurturing we receive in early life. Child development specialists have designed one experiment after another to study this question, pushing the pendulum of favor back and forth between nature and nurture.

Three decades ago, child psychiatrists Stella Chess and Alexander Thomas began the landmark research that is now widely regarded as proof that many of our character traits are inborn. They followed a group of 130 individuals with similar family backgrounds from early infancy into adulthood to see whether infant temperaments are permanent or changeable. After evaluating the babies in nine characteristics, including distractibility, attention span, persistence, activity level, and intensity of reaction, the researchers identified three basic character clusters, or temperament types: While a third of the sample did not fit any of these types, about 40 percent were "easy" babies, regular and predictable, able to adapt to new situations easily and cheerfully. Another 15 percent were "slow to warm up," with a low to moderate activity level; they were cautious in new situations and sometimes moody or unresponsive. And 10 percent qualified as "difficult" babies, irregular and intense in their responses, unwilling to adapt to new situations, and easily frustrated. These temperamental characteristics did not change or fade significantly over time. One startling finding, in fact, was that 70 percent of the difficult babies but only 18 percent of the easy babies developed problems requiring psychiatric attention in later life.[3]

Emmy Werner's study of the children of Kauai supports this finding. The children who were most resilient to abuse, poverty, and health and family problems during childhood, who became happy, well-adjusted grown-ups despite their troubled backgrounds, tended to have extremely engaging personalities. "Even as infants," writes Dr. Werner, "the resilient individuals were described by their parents as 'active,' 'affectionate,' 'cuddly,' 'easygoing' and 'eventempered.' They had no eating or sleeping problems that were distressing to those who took care of them."[4]

Werner's study suggests that the temperaments we are born with set us up, in a way, for certain experiences and responses from other people, including our families. Any parent knows that it is difficult and sometimes impossible to maintain an even, understanding, and tolerant demeanor—to be the ideal, "functional" parent—around a child who persistently whines or cries inconsolably. And sometimes a clear display of parental anger is the only way to persuade a very stubborn child to stop running out into traffic or otherwise endangering himself. On the other hand, children who are naturally happy, even-tempered, and self-reliant tend to have fewer problems with their parents, teachers, and friends because they are, quite literally, easy to love. What happens, then, is that nurture reinforces nature.

Temperaments also act as filters for our experiences and reactions, so that our perceptions of early childhood are defined as much by our own inborn personalities as by actual events. A sharp reprimand to one child may reduce her to tears, while the same exact comment in the same tone of voice will leave a child with a less intense temperament unfazed. The sensitive child may later recall the incident as traumatic, while the more easygoing probably won't remember it at all. According to Jerome Kagan, professor of developmental psychology at Harvard, "The temperamental variations among young children imply that there will be few uniform consequences of a particular class of experience. Each child's temperament leads him or her to impose a special frame on experience, thus making it difficult to predict the consequences of a particular home environment."[5] This is an extremely important point, because it throws open the whole interpretation of dysfunction in families and other relationships. Much of the "emotional abuse" that self-help leaders like Bradshaw claim identifies the dysfunctional family may, in fact, be the retrospective product of the "victims'" own temperament.

One of my patients, a small, shy, soft-spoken woman in her forties named Laura, described in vivid terms the emotional abuse that her father had inflicted on her. Laura had come to me because she suffered from panic attacks, which she was convinced were a reaction against the way her father had treated her. He was hypercritical of both her and her twin sister, she told me. Nothing they or their mother did was ever good enough. He said things like, "Is that the best you can do?" and "I don't want to see you until you get it right," which made her feel demeaned.

About three weeks after Laura began therapy, her twin sister, Jenny, visited from out of town, and Laura asked to include her in our session. It was immediately evident that they were not identical twins. Her sister was big-boned, held herself very erect, and spoke in a loud, booming voice. She introduced herself right away and gripped my hand firmly in greeting. Her presence filled the entire room, while Laura's huddled in a corner of the couch.

As Laura and Jenny began to talk about their father it was almost impossible to believe that they were describing the same person. What Laura considered verbal abuse, Jenny had always thought of as constructive criticism. While Laura had been intimidated by her father's demands for improvement, Jenny had appreciated them because, she said, "It made me realize that you can always do better, that there really is no such thing as perfect. All Dad ever said was that we could stop when we'd done a good enough job, but we shouldn't pretend that what we'd done was perfect. And I think that's exactly right!"

The critical difference between Laura and her sister was not that their parents had loved one better than the other or given them different messages in raising them. Since they were twins, the difference could have nothing to do with birth order. And neither woman had experienced any significant life traumas that would have seriously altered her self-esteem. The primary reason that one was in therapy and the other never had been, that one viewed her childhood as "dysfunctional" while the other considered it better than average, was that they had such different temperaments. Jenny had been born cheerful, outgoing, and relatively at ease with herself, while her sister had never been able to accept the feelings of shyness and anxiety that were part of her innate makeup.

Since we can't significantly change our personalities, we have to learn to live with them, and we'll live with them more comfortably if we can figure out how they affect the way we think, feel, and behave. In his work with relapsed alcoholics, psychologist Emil Chiauzzi has identified five basic character traits that seem to promote addiction and inhibit recovery.[6]

• *Compulsiveness* makes people perfectionistic, very orderly, and reluctant to express their feelings. Unable to admit how hard it is to control their drinking, compulsive people will often interpret a minor slip as a major failure, which may, in turn, trigger a full-blown relapse.

• *Dependency* interferes with decision making and makes it hard for people to initiate or take responsibility for their actions. It also inhibits change, so that dependent alcoholics often cling to others who will help them quit drinking initially but cannot free themselves to take control of their own lives. When they discover that their rescuers will not assume this control for them, they often turn again to alcohol for comfort.

• *Passive-aggressive tendencies* make it difficult for people to express their feelings directly. Instead, they may complain, manipulate, make excuses, or procrastinate. If others confront them directly, they may feel threatened and back away from their accosters, even if it means leaving therapy or turning away from people who are trying to help them. The resulting frustration and isolation sends them back to drinking.

• *Narcissism* locks people into a self-image that is too good to be true and makes it difficult for them to accept constructive criticism. People who have narcissistic tendencies feel that they are entitled to special treatment and unconditional acceptance, which means that they usually wind up in rather superficial relationships. As alcoholics, they may pretend that they are not addicted or, if they are in treatment, that it doesn't matter if they relapse occasionally.

• *Antisocial tendencies* make it difficult for alcoholics to admit when they need help. Instead, they may alienate themselves from therapists and others who might help by trying to manipulate or overpower them. Convinced that they can solve their problems without help, they may be so enraged by failure that they either give up the effort to recover or punish themselves by retreating back into addiction.

Working through such character patterns does not necessarily mean eliminating them. If you have a compulsive personality, you probably are not capable of becoming as laid-back as someone born with an easygoing nature. It would be futile to pin your recovery on that expectation. But you can learn to moderate your compulsiveness and communicate your true feelings, and you can develop constructive outlets for the frustration that occurs when you make mistakes. Once you see how your feelings, attitudes, and behavior blend into a recognizable pattern, you can also avoid situations in which you are likely to feel overly frustrated or anxious. The key is to acknowledge your basic temperament and work *with* it as you work toward change.

YOUR CULTURAL MIX

The self-help movement's preoccupation with family dysfunction ignores not only our innate qualities but also the cultural influences that affect our lives. Each generation, ethnic group, school, religion, profession, and geographic area has its own culture. And each culture imposes certain values and expected modes of behavior on its members. Some of these cultural standards cultivate personal problems, including addiction and victimization, while others mitigate against them.

Researcher George Vaillant found that alcoholism occurs seven times more frequently among Irish men than among men from Mediterranean cultures. The Irish, he explained, "tend to forbid alcohol before age 21, to admire drunkenness among men, and to drink outside the home and apart from meals," while in Mediterranean cultures, "children are taught to drink by their parents, drinking occurs with meals, and drunkenness is taboo."[7] He also found that the Irish tend to see drinking as a black-and-white issue rather than as an issue of moderation. When they become alcoholics, they are more likely to succeed in AA's program of total abstinence than are their Italian counterparts, who have more success in moderating their consumption than abstaining completely. The Irish culture, like AA, draws a line between not drinking and drinking. Among Italians, by contrast, the line is between controlled drinking and drunkenness.

In the Jewish and Chinese communities, as well, the focus is on self-control rather than abstinence, and resulting rates of alcoholism are far below those of most other cultural groups. The Jewish aversion to drunkenness is embodied in the phrase "*shikker* [drunk] as a goy." The Chinese attitude is reflected in sociologist Milton Barnett's findings that among the 15,515 arrests made in New York's Chinatown between 1933 and 1949, not one was for public drunkenness. "While drinking was socially sanctioned," wrote Barnett, "becoming drunk was not. The individual who lost control of himself under the influence of liquor was ridiculed and, if he persisted in his defection, ostracized."[8]

In all these cases, it is the community as well as the family that imposes cultural values and attitudes. Young Jews, Italians, and Chinese are likely to control their drinking as much because their peers and neighbors disapprove of drunkenness as because their parents have taught them self-restraint. Within their cultures, their social life, educational and employment opportunities, and marital prospects all depend on their good comportment, with no excuses made for the "disease" of addiction. Because the stakes are an integral part of the social structure, are clear up front and are presented in terms of personal responsibility rather than an ineffable sickness, young people in these communities do not easily slide into addiction.

In our assimilated society, of course, most of us belong to multiple cultures, which sometimes send conflicting messages. When a young boy raised in Chinatown goes away to a mainstream American college, he may be caught between the fraternity culture, which encourages excessive drinking, and the Chinatown culture that has taught him moderation. Which influence rules him may be determined by his temperament; if naturally wary and cautious, he will probably resist the fraternity influence, but if he is easily influenced and eager to please his new friends, he may go along with the drinking. Over time, the two cultures will both influence his personal values and beliefs, just as his family does.

The problem with this assimilation is that we may not be conscious of our cultural values. We may not realize how strong they are. We may not understand how they affect our attitudes and behavior. For example, if you have an Italian, or Jewish, or Chinese background and you turn to AA for help with a drinking problem, you may well feel uncomfortable with the program, but you might not understand why. The most likely reason is that your culture has trained you to view drinking not as a disease but as a matter of personal and moral responsibility.

It has conditioned you to treat alcohol as a substance over which you have control, not as a force over which you are powerless. And it has encouraged you to rely on self-restraint to moderate your consumption, not to abstain completely. In fact, what you call a drinking problem might not be a dependency at all but a loss of face over getting drunk on one or two occasions. If you do not make the connection between your cultural conditioning and your difficulty in accepting the Twelve Steps, you may feel that you have failed by quitting the program. And you may be baffled to discover that you actually are able to solve your problem by moderating your consumption. If, on the other hand, you are fully aware of your cultural values, you can rely on them to gauge the severity of your problems and to shape a recovery plan that can really work for you.

SOCIOPOLITICS

Other issues that are routinely ignored by most self-help leaders include money, sex, race, and political power. It is all well and good to unravel the personal and interpersonal conflicts that have been holding you back, but that may not significantly improve the quality of your life if you're struggling to get by on an unfair divorce settlement, if you live in an area with a depressed economy and can't find a job, if you can't find adequate childcare to enable you to work, or if your employer discriminates against you because you're a woman or nonwhite. Insecure women are the target audience for the codependence message, and two of the key factors in women's insecurity are economic dependence and the inequitable burden of childcare, yet the formula for "recovery" proposed by codependence leaders does nothing to help women secure equitable wages or quality childcare. Instead, it exhorts women to "forgive" themselves, "have a love affair with" themselves, "feel their own feelings," and "learn the art of acceptance." In effect, it urges them to *ignore the external situations* that are making their lives untenable.

To dwell on the tragic legacy of your dysfunctional family

without acknowledging the real, practical obstacles that you face today is a little like working over a leaky pipe while the house burns down around you. It may take your mind off the larger issues. It may give you the illusion of progress, the satisfaction of confronting that one problem. But you run the risk of dying in the fire, and, even if you survive, you'll be left with far worse problems than a leaky faucet.

Unfortunately, the "work" done in many self-help groups can be more of a distraction from real problems than a solution. And, in cases such as Miriam's, it is an expensive luxury.

I could tell from the way Miriam walked into my office for our first session that she was an angry woman. A permanent scowl was etched into her wide, dark face. She spoke in clipped, biting phrases, usually with an edge of sarcasm, and pushed her large body around as if it were a burden she resented having to carry.

"I never knew from a functional family," she said. "Never saw my father. My mother had three kids by three different men, and worked twelve, thirteen hours a day to stay off welfare. She was too proud to stay home with us, too overworked to ever really know us. We got dumped with a neighbor who already had five kids. She had us watch TV all day to keep us quiet, and fed us junk. Every one of us grew up fat."

Miriam's mother was a tough taskmaster, making sure her children knew how hard she worked and pushing them to excel in school in exchange for her sacrifices. Miriam didn't have much difficulty staying at the top of her class, but the Southern, mostly segregated schools that she attended did little to prepare her academically or socially for college. Although she got into a state university, she flunked out after one semester and got a job as a secretary. She was so humiliated that she didn't tell her mother until the end of the year. Over the next decade, she gained eighty pounds and went through six different employers. Finally, at a co-worker's suggestion, she joined Overeaters Anonymous where she learned that she ate because of low self-esteem instilled in her by her family. She stopped berating herself and began to feel her anger. She got angry at her father for not being there, at her mother for neglecting and pushing her, at her sister and brother for their indifference to her, at the woman who babysat her for her laziness and ignorance.

OA had taught Miriam to believe that her family had oppressed her instead of acknowledging the ways in which she'd been oppressed by institutional racism and poverty. It encouraged her to remember all the small cruelties her mother had inflicted out of desperation for her daughter to make a better life for herself, but not the effect that TV shows about rich white people had had on her. Not the way she'd recoiled when white boys yelled racial epithets at her. Not the moment she realized that being a star pupil at a black school meant nothing on a white campus. Not the countless subtle digs at her intelligence by employers who just didn't believe that blacks were really as smart as whites. Miriam was right to be angry, but her family was not the monster. And until she began to confront the wider social and political forces that had made her and her family "dysfunctional" she was not likely to make much real progress with her weight or her inner turmoil.

Miriam's case demonstrates that not all personal problems can be solved through psychotherapy or self-help programs alone. It may help to understand yourself, to be more assertive with your family and friends, to express your feelings openly. But you may also need to work on changing the *situations* that are holding you back. This may involve political or legal action. It may mean moving to a more welcoming or safer environment. It may require a career change. It could also mean joining community groups, such as Neighborhood Watch, day-care organizations, or school associations, which have nothing to do with personal recovery—except that they are absolutely vital for *your* personal recovery.

THE INVENTORY OF SIGNIFICANT LIFE EVENTS

One of AA's Twelve Steps is to make "a searching and fearless moral inventory of ourselves." The idea is to go within and make a list of all our good and bad habits, attitudes, feelings, and behaviors and to see how they have contributed to our problems. This is a good exercise for assessing temperament, but it doesn't go far enough. It doesn't help us separate the attitudes that we were born with from the attitudes that are learned. It doesn't identify the outside influences that have shaped the way we feel about ourselves and others. And it doesn't help us understand how we fit into the broader contexts of family, community, and society.

There is another exercise that will give you this broad perspective on yourself and your life. It is called the Inventory of Significant Life Events.

1. Think of the events—conversations, experiences, moments of realization—that have had the most significant impact on your feelings about yourself today. Include both the events that have affected you positively and those that have had a negative impact. To help organize these events, list them under the appropriate heading below. Don't worry if some headings have no events listed, while others have many. The timeline should include only significant events, and these won't necessarily fall into an even pattern.

RATING

Preschool childhood: _____ _____

_____ _____

_____ _____

TOTAL _____

Age 5–13

Family life: _____ _____

_____ _____

_____ _____

TOTAL _____

RATING

School and social life: _____ _____

_____ _____

_____ _____

TOTAL _____

Age 14–18

Family life: _____ _____

_____ _____

_____ _____

TOTAL _____

School and social life: _____ _____

_____ _____

_____ _____

TOTAL _____

Adulthood

College experiences: _____ _____

_____ _____

_____ _____

TOTAL _____

Sex and romance: _____ _____

_____ _____

_____ _____

TOTAL _____

RATING

Work experiences: _____ _____

_____ _____

_____ _____

                                        TOTAL _____

Community and social interactions: _____ _____

_____ _____

                                        TOTAL _____

Parenthood: _____ _____

_____ _____

_____ _____

                                        TOTAL _____

Relationship with parents and siblings: _____ _____

_____ _____

_____ _____

                                        TOTAL _____

Health problems: _____ _____

_____ _____

_____ _____

                                        TOTAL _____

If you are having difficulty pinpointing your significant events, the following examples might help:

Family events might include the death or divorce of parents, or physical or emotional abuse.

School events might include incidents of academic excellence or failure, humiliating school experiences, extremely supportive or extremely antagonistic teachers.

Romantic events might include your first sexual experience, particularly painful breakups or unrequited love affairs, marriage, divorce, or the death or illness of a lover.

Community-related events might include incidents of racial or religious persecution, sexual harassment, or political activities.

2. How did each of the events you listed affect the way you view yourself today? For each entry you made, rate the event according to the following scale in the space provided:

> + 2 Very positively
> + 1 Somewhat positively
> − 1 Somewhat negatively
> − 2 Very negatively

Example: You might consider the event in the following way: I was extremely humiliated by the hazing that I went through when I joined a fraternity in college. At the time, I felt demeaned and humiliated by it, but it made me rethink my attitudes about these social institutions and the way they seemed to reward abuses of power. I dropped out of my fraternity and ended up feeling stronger, more independent, and self-confident as a result. Even though the hazing affected me negatively at the time, I would give it a somewhat positive (+ 1) rating in this exercise because of the way I view it today.

3. Tally up the scores under each heading. By comparing the different totals for each group you can tell:

- Which periods of your life had the greatest positive or negative impact on you.
- Which influences on your life (e.g., family, school, work, or romance) have had the greatest positive or negative impact on you.

This inventory illustrates how many different facets there are to your life, how many different experiences have contributed to the person you are today. One of the major tasks of recovery is to recognize these different dimensions and build on the positive, while learning enough from the negative events to put them behind you and prevent their recurrence. The next few chapters will give you the information and tools you need to accomplish this task.

NOTES

1. John Bradshaw, "Our Families Ourselves: Loneliness of the Lost Child," *Lear's* (November 1989): p. 87.

2. Skip Hollandsworth, "The Codependency Conspiracy," *Texas Monthly* (February 1990): 136.

3. Jane and Joseph Jackson, *Infant Culture* (New York: Crowell, 1978), pp. 191–94.

4. Emmy Werner, "Children of the Garden Island," *Scientific American* (April 1989): 108D.

5. Jerome Kagan, *The Nature of the Child* (New York: Basic Books, 1984), p. 70.

6. Emil Chiauzzi, "Breaking the Patterns That Lead to Relapse," *Psychology Today* (December 1989): 18–19.

7. George Vaillant, *The Natural History of Alcoholism* (Cambridge, Mass.: Harvard University Press, 1983), p. 61.

8. Stanton Peele, *The Diseasing of America* (Lexington, Mass.: Lexington Press, 1989). p. 72.

CHAPTER 6

Remember the Past, Don't Live It

Your past is comprised of memories—good, bad, and neutral—which can be part of your life or overrun it, depending on how you deal with them. If you've been involved in traditional psychoanalysis or the codependence movement, you have been taught that your current problems are inextricably connected to past traumas and that you cannot recover without analyzing these old hurts. While I don't deny that there is a connection between past and present or that it can help immensely to understand this connection, I am concerned that much of the "analysis" that occurs, particularly in self-help programs, mistakes distorted memories for facts.

In order to understand ourselves, where we've come from and where we're heading, we must challenge our memories. I realize that this is the same advice that codependence leaders gave Skip Hollandsworth in the last chapter; most self-help programs do instruct followers to challenge the past. But they only question the past that's remembered as being neutral or positive. If you can't recall or if, like Hollandsworth, you think your early life was basically okay, then you're told you're in denial and must dredge up the painful truth. If you assert that your past was miserable, however, you are automatically entitled to empathetic support, no questions asked. This double standard reflects the bias of the self-help movement to dwell on and embellish trauma even at the expense of emotional health. It ignores the fact that all memory is distorted, that we may deny or downplay the positive as well as the negative elements of our past lives. I believe that we have to challenge *all* our memories to yield an accurate reading of history.

Once we've identified what really happened to make us the way we are, we have to use effective methods to put the past firmly behind us. Unfortunately, this is another area where the self-help and psychoanalytic approaches are woefully inadequate. They encourage obsession with the past and provide few constructive suggestions for resolving or overcoming ancient wounds. It's a bit like trying to drive a car forward while looking only in the rearview mirror. You don't get very far that way, and you run the risk of a crack-up. I prefer to check the rear view from time to time, making sure that the reflection is accurate, but concentrate most of my attention on the road ahead. Only if I see something gaining on me from behind do I stop to deal with it. Otherwise, I remind myself that most of what appears in my rear view will soon be gone, but the road ahead is always presenting new and meaningful challenges.

CONFRONT THE DISTORTIONS

We all view our lives through layers of distortions. Our most vivid memories rarely reflect the way things really were, and most don't even reflect the way we actually felt at the moment. That's why old home movies are always full of surprises. People and places rarely look on film the way we remember them. The scale seems all wrong. The atmosphere doesn't feel right. But is film or memory more reliable?

Admittedly, home movies tell only part of the story, but that part is objective and unchanging. Memories, on the other hand, change constantly. And, in the changing, they are distorted by time, by our own limited perspective, by other people's suggestions, and by our own desire to replay the past in a particular way.

Distortions of Time

Time has a polarizing effect on our view of the past. It separates our experiences into good and bad categories in much the same way that distance makes us see our surroundings as blocks of light and dark. In both cases, neutral details are obscured or absorbed into one extreme or the other. As time passes, our positive memories seem to grow lighter and more wonderful, while the negative ones become darker and more painful. By the time twenty or thirty years have elapsed, all we have left are scenes that either fill our hearts with sweet nostalgia or fill our souls with rage.

If you could count on an even balance between nostalgia and rage, this dichotomy might be all right. However, another trick of time is to play games with the balance. Two years after your mother dies, you may remember her as two-thirds tyrant and one-third saint. But over time, even as the accuracy and detail of your memories fade, you may *feel* more strongly about them. It is confusing and frustrating if your feelings about related memories conflict with each other, so you may subconsciously adjust the memories to bring your emotions into agreement. Thus, ten years after your mother dies, instead of equivocating in your feelings about her, you may brand her a full-fledged tyrant, or maybe you'll conclude that your earlier assessment was wrong and anoint her an absolute saint. Either way, you will feel a natural pull to place her squarely in one camp or the other. It's not the facts that change over time but your need for a cohesive verdict.

Distortions of Perspective

We all have an extremely limited point of view. We cannot read each other's minds. We cannot step outside ourselves and watch our own behavior. We cannot live through anyone's experiences but our own. And, of course, because everyone suffers these limitations of perspective, no one else can read our minds, or see the world through our eyes, or experience life exactly the same way we do. This built-in one-sidedness means that all our perceptions, even of events that are taking place right before our eyes, are inherently distorted. The small child whose father slaps him knows only that he is hurt and insulted by what he views as an unprovoked attack. He cannot know that his father has just been laid off from his job and is worried that he may not have enough money to support the family more than a few months. The child, caught up in playing, does not realize that his father is just too exhausted and preoccupied to tolerate his shouting and constant demands for attention. Nor does he believe that when his father warned him to quiet down, he meant that he would be punished if he did not comply. The child's experience tells him simply that he's been abused.

Such distortions of perspective, unfortunately, tend to be magnified over time. Unless the child is informed of his father's crisis and develops some sympathy for him to balance his own hurt feelings, the slapping incident may well fester into a memory of monstrous mistreatment, exactly the kind of memory that codependence leaders point to as evidence of a dysfunctional childhood.

Distortions by Suggestion

Our interpretation of reality is frequently influenced by the feedback we get from others. Continuing the last example, the child's long-term memory of the slapping incident will be directly affected by the reactions of others when he tells them about it. If his mother is outraged, he will think that his father's crime was even worse than he thought. If she admits that it was a mistake but makes him understand the circumstances, he may forgive his father. If she tells the child that he was to blame, then he may remember the incident as proof of his own worthlessness.

Whatever the child's conclusion, it will remain open to review as long as he can recall it well enough to describe to others. Thus, even if the grown child has long since decided that his father slapped him because he was upset about his job, when he recounts the event to a friend who accepts codependence theory he may end up with an entirely different interpretation of his past—most likely, an interpretation that portrays his father as an abuser who permanently scarred his child's inner self.

Because we are so suggestible, we may allow our memories to be completely reshaped by people who have impressive credentials or present themselves as experts. Such helpful persuasion often does more harm than good, as writer Lawrence Durrell pointed out in a passage in his novel *Clea* (one of his *Alexandria Quartet*). Durrell's character Justine had spent most of her adult life shuttling between European psychoanalysts who attempted to help her resurrect her memories of being sexually molested as a child. With their help, she had built the incident into a monstrous, insurmountable violation that had largely taken over her identity. Because the psychoanalysts were the experts, no one, least of all Justine, dared question their methods, until one of Justine's friends challenged not only the psychoanalysts but Justine's memories themselves. "You have wasted all this time," he told her, "trying to come to terms with an imaginary conception of damage done to you. Try dropping this invented guilt and telling yourself that the thing was both pleasurable and meaningless. Every neurosis is made to measure!" Justine was astonished: "It was curious that a few words like this, and an ironic chuckle, could do what all the others could not do for me. Suddenly everything seemed to lift, get lighter, move about."[1] Durrell was reacting against the methods of Freudian analysts circa 1940, but he might as well have been commenting on today's codependence movement.

Distortions for Convenience

Finally, some memories are inaccurate because we simply do not want to accept or deal with the truth. Sometimes this is because we do not want to face our own culpability. It is easier for a young man to blame his parents for emotionally abusing him than to admit that he really was a difficult, temperamental child. And sometimes we distort the past because we want to protect someone else. A woman may blame herself for causing her sister's death rather than acknowledge that her sister, whom she worshiped, was so disturbed that she took her own life.

Usually, though, we choose to accept distorted memories because we don't want to go through the work of identifying the truth. The distortions tend to give us easy answers. They generally make the past seem less complex than it really was. And they fit into the overall scheme of our lives. To confront our distortions of memory we must be willing to challenge our very identity.

CORRECT THE DISTORTIONS

Of course, this identity challenge is a fundamental part of recovery. It is virtually impossible to conquer chronic or critical problems without reinventing yourself to some degree. And this reinvention requires a careful reassessment of your past, which may involve using the following techniques to correct your distortions of memory. In general, you would use these techniques only to examine past events that are particularly painful or difficult to think about or that you cannot *stop* thinking about, but you might want to try them with a less critical incident just to check the overall accuracy of your memory.

1. Ask yourself how and why you are recycling this memory. If you are haunted or obsessed by a particular memory or set of memories, you may be exaggerating the relative importance of the past. Why would you do this? There are several possible reasons:

If the memory is of something critical that has happened within the last six months, it is natural for it to be on the forefront of your mind. A recently concluded love affair or the death of a loved one may dominate your thoughts for weeks afterward.

There may be nothing you can do to change what's happened and the event may have had little effect on the general flow of your life, yet you need to keep turning it over in your mind for a while to come to terms with it. There is nothing unusual or unhealthy about such grieving periods. In fact, they are often necessary to complete the emotional adjustment after a trauma. But if the preoccupation persists beyond six months to a year or more, or if it resurfaces years later, then you must ask yourself why you can't get past it.

You may discover that the obsession fills a vacuum. You may be focusing on the past because you do not have enough going on in the present. Let's say you keep coming back to a childhood memory of a terrible family argument in which you were insulted and humiliated. You have traced your low self-esteem back to that argument. It has come to represent your family's mistreatment of you throughout your childhood. The question is, what have you done to improve your self-esteem in the intervening years? Low self-esteem does not have to be a permanent condition and won't be if you engage in activities that give you a sense of mastery and accomplishment. But you may find that it's easier to keep worrying this memory and blaming it for your past unhappiness than it is to go out and do something about your *present* unhappiness. If this is your choice, so be it, but be honest with yourself and admit that you have chosen this preoccupation. You were not condemned to it.

You may also be recycling the past because it brings you certain rewards. When you describe your memory of this horrible family scene in which you were the abused child, most of your listeners will react sympathetically. They are attentive. They say they admire your ability to survive. They may forgive certain weaknesses in you. They may welcome you into their self-help group. And they may make it difficult for you to put that family scene behind you. In this case, you probably will need to disengage from the group to disengage from the past. You may also need to take a closer look at the memory itself.

2. Consider the circumstances surrounding the remembered event. As you think about a particular incident, try to fit it into context. Broaden the focus from what you were doing or feeling to what was going on around you. As you reconstruct this family argument, ask yourself what prompted the dispute. Which members of your family were involved? How old was each person at the time? What else was going on in the family during the period surrounding the argument? How did the others react to the argument? Was that particular battle part of an ongoing family war or was it a singular event? Did it cause any significant changes to occur afterward? By looking at the surrounding events and conditions, you may change your view of the argument's relative importance or significance.

3. Check the records. Once you have traced your memory to a particular time and setting, collect as much outside information about the event as you can. Look for documents from around that time. Compare your memories of the incident with those of others who were there. Returning to our example of the family blow-up, you might examine old photographs to see if you can detect in the faces of your family any traces of the emotions that you associate with the argument. If the police were called in to break up the dispute, you might find an official report on the incident. Or perhaps someone in the family wrote about the fight in a note or letter. Even if there is no documentation, you can poll the other family members to see if you all agree about the severity and significance of the argument. If you do not agree, you may need to find out if there are relevant facts that the others know and you don't.

4. Turn the tables on yourself. Think about the part you played in the event you are remembering. Were you an active participant or an observer? What did the other players think you were doing? How did they react to you? This is a particularly important exercise if memory casts you as the victim. Let's say that this family argument that has been haunting you for years concluded with your mother screaming at you and storming out of the house. Try to put yourself in your mother's place. Consider her general personality, her relationship with your father, the other pressures she was under at the time. Think about your overall relationship with her. Now look at yourself through her eyes. Look at the way you behaved during the argument. Listen to what you said to her. Try to imagine what she felt when she screamed at you, what prompted her to leave. You may still believe that she was in the wrong, that you were the innocent, but you also may begin to see that other conclusions are possible.

5. Challenge your advisers. Trace the course of your memory back to the time when it first started to bother or preoccupy you. It is possible that you've been wrestling with this memory ever since the original event, but that's unlikely if the event took place many years ago. Usually there is a kind of black-out period after a significant incident when you simply don't think about it. Codependence leaders call this the period of denial, but I call it normal. You push back the memory so that you can deal with the other things that are going on in your life. Sometimes you push it back because it is too painful, sometimes because there is simply nothing to gain by dwelling on it. Such so-called denial can be a healthy defense.

When something or someone in the present jogs the memory, it will return, but not necessarily in its original form. Such promptings can color your memory, put a new twist or interpretation on it. For this reason, you need to ask yourself *why* you have suddenly started to think about this particular event. What was going on in your life when the memory came back to you? Were you in therapy or in a self-help program? Did someone challenge you to call up the past? Did you relate the event to something that you were studying or had just learned? If you find that you've been thinking about this family argument because it proves your counselor's theory that you came from a dysfunctional family, you might do well to ask how your counselor arrived at this theory in the first place. Did she make a thorough assessment of you and your personal history before arriving at this theory? Or does she start with the assumption that everyone has a dysfunctional background and then look for the specifics to prove it? Did she have to convince you that this argument was a significant event in your life? How would she react if you told her that you had concluded the incident was meaningless?

We all are vulnerable to what I call the "Aha" Factor. "Aha, that explains it," we say when someone hands us a theory that seems to fit our experience. The thrill of self-recognition and the relief of a ready answer are so powerful that we tend to accept rather than challenge the theory, even when it is full of holes. The "Aha" Factor is largely responsible for the popularity of the codependence movement, because the movement is made to reflect virtually everyone's experience. But just because we can all identify with certain experiences does not mean that our experiences occurred for the same reasons or that we were all affected by these experiences in exactly the same way. It is all too easy to distort our memories to suit someone else's designs. To prevent this from happening, we must challenge those designs.

CONFRONT THE PAST

What if your investigation concludes that you had reason to be traumatized by something that happened in the past? What if, even after challenging your memories, you remain obsessed with them?

It is not possible to change what happened to you, and it is probably not possible to avenge past traumas. But by confronting those who have wronged you, by openly expressing your feelings toward them, and by changing the way you deal with them from now on, *you can release yourself from the past*. This confrontation can take the form of a face-to-face meeting, letter, role play, or imaginary dialogue. Whatever form it takes, you need to cover the following points:

1. Describe the particular event as you remember it.
2. Describe how you felt about it at the time.
3. Explain how you think the event has affected you, why you are having difficulty letting go of the memory.

4. Describe how you plan to put the memory behind you and what you want from the other person now and in the future.

Face-to-face confrontation is possible only if you know the person who wronged you and can arrange a safe meeting. Do not try to reason in person with someone you suspect will react violently. And do not attempt a personal confrontation without giving careful thought ahead of time to what you will say. Make a pact with yourself to remain calm, express your honest feelings, and not let yourself be controlled or manipulated. Your goal is to release your own feelings and, ideally, to initiate a new policy for dealing with this person in the future, but don't assume or even expect that the other person will be sympathetic. Here is an example of one way the conversation might go if you confronted your mother about attacking and abandoning you during that family argument:

YOU: I need to talk to you about something that happened a long time ago, something we've never really discussed. Something that's disturbed me since I was sixteen. That night you and Dad started arguing about whether or not we had enough money for me to go to college. Do you remember? You said you didn't want to waste it on me because I was too stupid to do anything useful with my life. You wanted to save the money for another two years so that Davey could go, because he was the only one in the family who had any real brains. Dad said if you hadn't wasted so much money on clothes there would be enough for school for us both, and then you flew into a rage. I started to cry, and you screamed at me to get out of your way, then you left and didn't come home for two days.

MOTHER: Oh, now really, you've blown the whole thing way out of proportion. It was an argument between me and your father. It had nothing to do with you.

YOU: You may remember it that way, but I am not exaggerating. Dad and Davey remember it exactly as I do. Ever since that night I have believed that I am

115

stupid and worthless. Hearing you say those things convinced me that you'd never loved me and never would.

MOTHER: I loved you. I do now. But it's always been difficult for me to express affection. I never knew how to talk to you. We never had any common ground.

YOU: It's unfortunate that you were so repressed, but I think you should realize how you made me feel. The things you said to me that night were cruel and unwarranted.

MOTHER: I'm sorry. I never meant to be cruel to you.

YOU: If you really mean that, I'll accept the apology. But I want more. I want a relationship with you, but it has to be based on mutual respect. I want you to stop prejudging everything I do. I want you to acknowledge the positive things I've done in my life. I want you to treat me like an adult.

Imaginary dialogue, role play, and the confrontational letter are useful devices if the other person is dead or otherwise unavailable, or is too violent to confront directly. A letter can also be used as a preliminary approach to a meeting. In either case, you need to cover the same four confrontational points. You will ask for change and invite a response, but the primary purpose of the confrontation, especially if you are addressing someone who has died, is to acknowledge your experience and vent your feelings. Here is a confrontational letter that a patient named Veronica wrote to her boyfriend, Sandy, ten years after he committed suicide:

Dear Sandy,

   I need to tell you how I remember the night you died. I remember you laughing. I remember you lying to me. I remember you telling me that you loved me more than anything. I remember you abandoning me. You promised me that everything was going to be all right, and then you deserted me. You betrayed me.

I have had a lot of trouble forgiving you for that night, Sandy. You were in trouble, and you never let me get close enough to help. Ever since you died, I've been too afraid to get seriously involved with anyone else. Afraid of being locked out again. Afraid of being lied to. Afraid of being abandoned. Afraid of that horrible sense of uselessness and dread that closed over me after you were gone.

But now I'm tired of living my life afraid. I'm ready to change, and I need you to know how angry and hurt you made me feel. I need you to understand how much I cared about you. Yes, that I loved you! I want to remember you from now on with love, not pain.

You will always be part of me, Sandy, but I cannot let you control me any more. I'm going to store your memory away in a special place in my heart where you'll be safe, protected, but where you cannot hurt me. It's time to stop the hurting.

Good-bye.

RECONCILE THE PAST AND PRESENT

After you have come to terms with the emotions unleashed by old memories, you may need to check and see whether your past experiences have affected your patterns of behavior or belief. Veronica's reluctance to enter a new romantic relationship is a good example of this kind of patterning. The memory of Sandy's death was like a lens through which Veronica saw all men. Each time she met someone new, no matter how different he was from Sandy, she imagined that he would abandon or reject her. And even after she had finally put Sandy's memory to rest, she had to work against the pattern that had been established over the previous decade. She had to consciously push herself to accept each new man as an individual, not to brand him out of habit.

As you start to adjust a particular behavior or belief pattern, keep in mind how your life has changed since that pattern originated. In Veronica's case, she was now ten years older and vastly more independent than she had been when Sandy died. At age twenty she had longed for an intense, dramatic relationship that swept her off her feet. One of the reasons she had such difficulty relinquishing Sandy's memory was that she believed the two of them might have had the relationship she longed for. And yet, once she had finally come to terms with his death, she was quite astonished to realize that she now wanted an entirely different kind of relationship. She wanted commitment, reliability, someone who would make a loving husband and a good father for her future children. Someone completely different from Sandy. In fact, she had to admit that if she'd met Sandy today, she would not choose to get involved with him. This realization was Veronica's proof that she had finally broken through the destructive legacy of her lover's death.

Remember the past, don't live it. Recognize that it is part of your life, and yet is separate from the present. It has contributed to the person you are today, but is not your entire identity. And while your memories may yield some insights into your feelings, attitudes, and behavior, they will not necessarily give you a magic key to recovery. That magic depends on your ability to move beyond the realm of memory and accept responsibility for your life, here and now.

CHALLENGE YOUR PAST

How well do you manage your past? The following exercise will help you determine the accuracy of your memories and the extent to which they affect your present life.

1. Rate your ten most compelling memories. List the ten memories that you think about most often or that you think have made the biggest impact on your identity. These might include

significant life events, such as the death of a sibling or parent, or more general memories, such as a recurrent dream you had when you were very young.

MEMORY   **RATING**

1. _____ _____
2. _____ _____
3 _____ _____
4. _____ _____
5. _____ _____
6. _____ _____
7. _____ _____
8. _____ _____
9. _____ _____
10. _____ _____

TOTAL (sum of ratings divided by 10) _____

Now, in the column provided, rate your feelings about each of these memories, according to the following scale:

1 = Very positive
2 = Somewhat positive
3 = Somewhat negative
4 = Very negative

The death of someone you loved would probably receive a very negative rating of 4, while the memory of your mother singing you to sleep as a child might receive a very positive rating of 1.

Total the ratings of all your memories and divide by 10. Compare this score to the rating scale above to determine whether you tend to remember mostly positive or negative aspects of the past.

2. Rate the accuracy of your memories. Look at the statements below and think of the ten memories on your list. For each memory give yourself a score of 1 by each statement that describes your recollection of that memory.

MEMORY									
1	2	3	4	5	6	7	8	9	10

This memory is very clear, like a highly detailed picture in my mind.

I've described this memory to others who were present at the time, and they remember it just as I do.

Photographs show the event exactly as I remember it.

Written records describe the event just as I remember it.

MEMORY

1	2	3	4	5	6	7	8	9	10

TOTALS

This memory has always been the same; no matter how many times I describe it or how many people try to reinterpret it for me, it never changes.

Total your score for each memory. A score of 2 or more suggests that your memory is probably very accurate. A score of 0–1 suggests that the memory may be weak or have some distortion.

3. Rate the impact of each memory on your present life. On page 122, under the appropriate column, rate the impact that each memory has on your life *now*. Answer each question according to the following numerical scale:

1 = Rarely
2 = Frequently
3 = Constantly

MEMORY	1	2	3	4	5	6	7	8	9	10	
											How often do you think about this memory?
											How often do you talk about this memory?
											How often do you feel distressed by this memory?
											How often does this memory distract you from other thoughts or activities?
											How often does this memory interfere with your relationships with others?
											How often does this memory cause you to behave in ways that you otherwise would not?
											TOTALS

Now add up your scores for each memory on your list and locate the total on the score sheet below.

Score   Evaluation

14–18   This memory is having a negative impact on your life. You are overly preoccupied with it, and it is interfering with your normal functioning. If you cannot move past it using the techniques in this chapter, you may need to seek professional help in dealing with it.

10–13   This memory has a moderate impact on your life. You may be devoting more attention to it than it deserves. Review the techniques described in this chapter and try to get a little more perspective on this past event.

6–9   This memory has a marginal impact on your life. You basically have accepted it as part of your past but keep it separate from your current activities and concerns.

NOTES

1. Lawrence Durrell, *Clea* (New York: Dutton, 1961), p. 59.

CHAPTER 7

Accept Responsibility for Your Own Choices and Actions

When you accept the victim or addict label, you are saying that you are powerless over your problems and therefore have no responsibility for them; because you are not responsible, you do not possess the power to change. This attitude is a vital part of AA's Twelve Step model, which relies on a spiritual Higher Power to supply the controls that addicts believe they are missing, but it is not necessarily accurate or appropriate as a long-term strategy. On the contrary, most people can achieve complete recovery only if they accept the responsibility and power of their own choices.

It can be difficult to determine where fate, force, and necessity leave off and active choice begins, yet choice is an essential part of all our lives. True, no one has complete control over everything that happens, but no one whose intellectual and physical faculties are intact is completely helpless, either. The challenge is to understand our choices and learn to make them responsibly.

THE MYTH OF POWERLESSNESS

"If you think you have a problem, then you do."
"An addiction can only grow worse."
"Unless you get treatment, you'll die."
These are the crisis messages of the "helping" industries that treat today's addictions. They play on our feelings of insecurity and confusion. They pretend to offer outside solutions to problems that we can only solve ourselves. And they foster the myth that we do not choose to behave as we do but are victims of undesirable circumstances or behaviors.

I realized just how completely this myth undermines personal responsibility when Darla, a veteran of Overeaters Anonymous, came into my office decrying her family for sabotaging her. The family had decided to have take-out food for dinner. Darla's aunt, who was doing the ordering, knew that Darla was dieting and was careful to ask her to choose her own food. Darla requested a salad. When the full order was on the table, however, Darla helped herself to several of the other dishes that were not on her diet. When the meal was over and for days afterward, she was irate. "They showed no sensitivity at all," she insisted. "They never asked if I would mind if they ordered dishes I liked. Once the food was on the table, I couldn't help myself!" Darla's program had persuaded her not only that she had no responsibility for her actions but that if others didn't take responsibility *for* her, they must be trying to undermine her recovery. No wonder she slipped! She had little chance of reforming her eating patterns as long as she continued to project her problem onto others.

The myth of personal powerlessness stems from the assumption that physical and psychological dependency begins with the first drink, the first drug experience, or, in the case of co-dependency, the first abusive or dysfunctional relationship, and that, once dependency begins, the user is helpless to quit without outside help. According to Dr. George Vaillant, this assumption is not based on fact: "The testimonials of the Alcoholics Anonymous speakers . . . which suggest that alcohol abuse often begins after the alcoholic's first drink, were not confirmed in this [Vaillant's] prospective study. Rather, alcohol dependence appears very much to resemble tobacco dependence. Nobody 'has to smoke' after a few weeks of cigarette use."[1]

Yet this myth has long been a cornerstone of antidrug propaganda in this country. At the turn of the century, prohibitionists warned drinkers of the dire effects of "demon rum," and the 1936 film *Reefer Madness* showed marijuana creating a Jekyll and Hyde–like transformation of young people into lunatics. But, as with the boy who cried wolf, the initial wave of emergency hysteria created by these scare tactics was quickly followed by a backlash of skepticism among those who dared to try the drugs and discovered that the warnings were absurdly exaggerated. The Haight-Ashbury generation found *Reefer Madness* so laughable that it became a cult film and, as a result, some drug experts suggest, large numbers of young adults were unwilling to believe the government's warnings about cocaine in the 1970s and 1980s.

Still, the exaggeration continues, as if the bleak reality of substance addiction is not bad enough to serve as fair warning. In 1988 the National Institute on Drug Abuse estimated that there are nearly half a million regular crack users in this country, nearly 900,000 frequent cocaine users, and more than 13 million problem drinkers. More than 700,000 people are arrested each year for drug violations. Another 97,500 die as a result of alcohol-related medical conditions, accidents, suicides, or murders. And more than 32 million Americans are clinically obese, which puts them at an increased risk for diabetes, heart disease, cancer, and a host of related medical problems.

These are grim facts. But it is also a fact that use of all illicit drugs fell 37 percent between 1985 and 1988, with the steepest decline showing in cocaine use, where the number of monthly users dropped by 50 percent. The number of cocaine-related deaths fell 26 percent in 1989,[2] and consumption of hard alcohol in the United States hit a thirty-year low in the late 1980s.[3] According to Dr. Herbert Kleber, deputy director of the Office of National Drug Control Policy, there are three or four times as many people who occasionally use cocaine as there are chronic abusers or addicts. There are seven occasional drinkers for every one who becomes an alcoholic.[4] And approximately seven Americans eat moderately for every one who becomes obese. Not all people who engage in "addictive behaviors" become addicts, and not all people who become addicted stay addicted for life. One of the critical elements is choice.

THE POWER TO CHOOSE

If addiction is a disease, then it is a disease of choice. Addicts choose their drugs. And, in support of this choice, they frequently choose to associate with other users and to remain in situations that nourish their addictions. They choose the addicted lifestyle. They choose their outlook on life. And they choose whether and when to kick their addiction.

Yet addicts freely admit that their habits have caused them tremendous pain and losses. Why would anyone choose such torment? There are several possible reasons:

• They cannot differentiate between fate and choice. They believe that addiction is what life had in store for them, and they can do nothing to change their lot. "Everyone in my family is fat," said one of my patients, using this reasoning to explain why she was nearly one hundred pounds overweight. She refused to focus on the fact that her diet, *by choice*, was high fat, high salt, and high calorie.

• They cannot differentiate between force and choice. They do not believe that they have the strength to escape the circumstances or people who guided them into addiction. "He'll kill me if I leave him," said a woman who had a long history of relationships with abusive men. Her fear of her lover was justified, but she still had a variety of options, which included going to the authorities and moving out of town to physically distance herself from him. She had made a *choice* to stay with him based on the questionable assumption that she was safer with him than apart from him, but she refused to take responsibility for this choice.

• They cannot differentiate between necessity and choice.

They believe that their addiction meets a need that they cannot otherwise fulfill. When a ghetto drug user says he "needs" to get high, he means that he needs to find some relief from the conditions of poverty, some sense of gratification to offset the humiliation of unemployment and perhaps homelessness. He *chooses* the illusory relief and gratification that drugs provide rather than accepting the vastly more difficult challenge of working his way out of poverty, but he does not need drugs.

In each case, the addict may truly believe that he or she has no choice, but this very belief is a choice in and of itself. Recovery depends on our willingness to admit that we, as human beings, have a choice in virtually everything we do, think, or feel.

We've all used the phrase "I can't help it" at one time or another. My children frequently say this to me when I catch them at something they know they shouldn't be doing, such as eating too much candy or falling behind in their homework. They know perfectly well they do have a choice, but they think that if I think they don't, I'll let them off the hook. Claiming powerlessness is easier than owning up to responsibility.

I hear the same refrain among my patients, many of whom are depressed because they use drugs, mistreat their children or spouses, or keep getting involved in unsatisfying relationships. Unlike my children, most of them genuinely believe that they are powerless to change their patterns. They feel victimized, needy, and hopeless. They are ashamed of the messes their lives have become and of their failure to make them better. Yet the essential reason for saying "I can't help it" is the same for these adults as it is for my children: It is easier to abdicate than to accept responsibility for one's actions.

But in denying choice and surrendering responsibility, we lose the sense of meaning that makes life worth living. Perhaps the most vivid illustrations of this principle are the stories of Nazi death camp inmates. Despite being stripped of family, belongings, names, and even the faith that they would survive the day, some managed to maintain a sense of self and purpose while others just gave up. In *Man's Search for Meaning*, Dr.

Viktor Frankl, an internationally renowned psychiatrist, wrote of his internment at Auschwitz and Dachau:

> We who lived in concentration camps can remember the men who walked through the huts comforting others, giving away their last piece of bread. They may have been few in number, but they offer sufficient proof that everything can be taken away from man but one thing: the last of the human freedoms—to choose one's attitude in any given set of circumstances, to choose one's own way.[5]

Even when faced with the most profound suffering, Frankl observed, we must choose whether to accept that suffering as a test and possibly even a source of inner strength, or whether to surrender that inner self and vegetate. Frankl conceded that the majority of concentration camp prisoners chose the latter option. Later in the same book, he observed that many of today's drug users, in slipping into addiction, are making the same choice.

CONSEQUENCES

For every action there is a reaction. I learned this basic rule in seventh-grade science, but it is as true of human behavior as of chemistry experiments. So is its corollary: For every action there is an intended purpose or goal.

Each time we make a responsible choice, we measure our goals against all likely reactions, including good, bad, and neutral consequences.

Before choosing a college three thousand miles from home, the responsible student and parents will weigh their desire for a quality school against the likelihood that the student will experience homesickness and culture shock and perhaps run up long-distance phone bills and air fares. They will also consider the possibility that the change of scene may broaden the student's perspectives, and that he may be able to spend some time with relatives who live near the school.

Before choosing to have sex with a man she's just met, the responsible woman asks herself whether the encounter is really likely to be as satisfying as she imagines, and whether it is worth the risk that the man will disappoint or mistreat her, that her boyfriend will find out, that her friends will disapprove, or that she'll contract a sexually transmitted disease.

Before choosing to steal from an open cash drawer, the responsible man considers whether the thrill and the monetary gain would really give him the pleasure he imagines, and whether this would justify the risk that the store's owner would see him, that he'd be branded a thief, that he might have to serve time, or even that he might get away with it and be tempted to steal again.

Some choices take months or years to process, but most take just a split second. Every day we send thousands of options through the mixmasters of our minds and come up with specific decisions. We choose whether and when to get up each day, what to wear and eat and say, whether to act kind, neutral, or cruel toward others, whether to wring the best out of life or let it pass us by. We are responsible for these decisions even if we do not make them responsibly, even if we do not claim responsibility for the consequences.

Let me explain by going through some typical remarks that patients make to deflect responsibility:

"*I can't stop* criticizing people." The biting, judgmental words just seemed to roll off the woman's tongue. It was almost as if they had a life of their own. But, on closer examination, it turned out that harsh, often unwarranted criticism gave the woman a way to salve her insecurity. It put her in a position of superiority. It drove people away, which protected her from having to deal with them on any more intimate level. And because she spoke this way only to people she knew would not retaliate, it gave her a sense of power. In short, the woman's hypercritical behavior served her purposes, even though it also embarrassed and alienated her. She could stop if she decided to confront her underlying problems. She had that choice. For all her insecurity, she was still responsible for her conduct.

"*I didn't mean to* have a drink with that other woman." The drink in question had lasted three hours and brought the man home to his wife at one in the morning. The other woman had been introduced to him by a friend who was encouraging the man to get a divorce. He was aware that his wife was home alone. He knew she was likely to be worried that he was out late, that she would be even more worried if she knew that he was with another woman. He recognized the probable consequences of his action, but chose to go ahead anyway. He certainly did mean to have that drink. And he was responsible both for the night out and for the repercussions at home.

"*I'm impulsive.*" She had run up $5,000 on her credit card over the past month. She was already $20,000 in debt and earned only $20,000 a year. But when this woman saw something she wanted, the desire was so strong that it overwhelmed her common sense. The impulse was there, and it was powerful, but so were the inevitable negative consequences of her shopping sprees. It was her responsibility to consider both the impulse and the consequences each time she reached for her credit card. If the temptation was too great for her to handle, then it was her responsibility to cut up her credit card or stop carrying it. Her impulsive nature demanded that she exercise extra responsibility, but it did not excuse her. And it was not her destiny.

We all have impulses, but some of us manage them better than others. Addicts do not manage their impulses well. In fact, they allow their impulses to rule their lives. The primary reason is that they do not acknowledge the consequences of their impulses. When I ask a young heroin addict what he was thinking the first time he put a needle in his arm, he'll tell me, "Nothing." When I ask why he did it, he'll say, "I wanted to get high." When I ask if he considered whether he would get sick from the needle, or become addicted, or eventually regret the decision, he'll repeat, "I just wanted to get high!" When I ask if he realized that those were some of the possible consequences, he'll reply, "Yeah, I knew. I just didn't think about them." He knew, but he chose not to acknowledge them. As a result, he was not in control of his impulses. He had no power over them. And he had no power over his life.

SELF-EFFICACY

We generally choose a particular course of action because we believe we can succeed at it. This belief in our ability to achieve results is what psychologist Albert Bandura has dubbed *self-efficacy*. As well as being the driving force behind most of our behavior, it plays an important role in determining our identity and emotional well-being. The greater our self-efficacy, the more competent and attractive we feel, the higher we set our goals, and the more satisfying life seems. A strong sense of self-efficacy raises self-esteem.

Self-efficacy is determined by four variables:

Past accomplishments: If you have been warmly received by audiences in the past, you will be more likely to seek future lecture enagagements than if you've never done any public speaking.

Observation: If you have watched other public speakers and determined that you have the required skill, poise, and material, you will be more likely to get up on stage than if you conclude that your personality is completely different from theirs.

Outside persuasion: If your friends and family say that you have an impressive stage presence, you will probably be more eager to face an audience than if you've been discouraged from performing.

Emotional arousal: If the thought of addressing a large group of people fills you with excitement and pleasure, you will be more willing to take up public speaking than if the prospect triggers a cold sweat.

Because we naturally avoid activities at which we do not expect to succeed, repeated failures will cause us to set our sights lower and lower in search of something that we can do well.

Repeated failures can lower standards to such an extent, however, that we may begin making decisions based more on self-delusion or wishful thinking than true self-efficacy. The high school dropout and social misfit who agrees to peddle drugs may convince himself that he can become rich and powerful, but to protect this faith he must ignore the more realistic consequences of his actions—that he will be cheated, jailed, or murdered.

Depression, fear, and insecurity make success seem much less accessible, and therefore damage self-efficacy. The more setbacks we endure, the lower our self-esteem plunges and the poorer becomes the quality of judgment governing our actions. We may, for example, be attracted to drugs, such as cocaine, that create the illusion of self-efficacy while actually undermining the user's talent and success. If we conclude that we cannot succeed at anything except self-destructive activities, then we are likely to join the ranks of Frankl's surrendered selves.

Because the variables that determine self-efficacy are interconnected, even minor disappointments can snowball into major problems. These different influences, then, must be unraveled.

When Allison began therapy, she was extremely depressed about her career. After twelve years in the film industry, she found herself working as a clerical secretary, earning less money than at any time since she was eighteen. "I'm thirty-five years old and a complete failure," she moaned. She saw herself as a failure not because of anything she'd chosen to do but because she'd decided that she was meant to be a failure. "It's my karma," she said with a wan smile.

And yet Allison had started out with high expectations for success. She came from a family of accomplished artists, her father a composer, her mother a stage actress. Both had instilled in her the belief that she could accomplish anything she set her mind to. At the same time, their successes set a high standard that Allison automatically used to measure her achievements. Although she had received training in both music and drama, she decided to find her own niche in the arts rather than try to compete with her parents. "I liked singing and acting," she recalled. "I was actually pretty good and might have worked up to a decent career as an actress, but I had this idea that if I wasn't superb right off the bat, I'd never survive."

With her confidence only slightly damaged, Allison set her sights on film production. Her mother arranged for an internship with a director one summer during high school. By the end of that summer, Allison felt so sure of her eventual success that, against her parents' advice, she decided not to go to college. The director hired her to work as an assistant in his company, which led to a succession of positions that paid well but involved long hours and a great deal of travel and did not give her the creative or intellectual satisfaction that she associated with success.

Coming back from one particularly demanding film shoot, Allison felt so exhausted and discouraged, so convinced of her own inadequacy that she decided to get out of movie production. Her mother, trying to be supportive, told her, "Maybe you were never really cut out for this business." The remark sent Allison's self-esteem into a nosedive. She was terrified that she might not be cut out for any business, which made it impossible for her to broach a new profession. Her financial needs eventually forced her to go back to work, but instead of launching a new career she became a temporary secretary. She hated the work, felt demeaned by the pay cut, but was afraid to attempt a more demanding job. The lower the cycle dragged her spirits, the more difficult it was for her to regain the feelings of self-efficacy she needed to rebuild her self-esteem and her career.

Allison's depression and fearfulness and her feelings of low self-worth were not based on actual experience so much as on unrealistic standards for achievement and on a succession of radical decisions that limited her chances of success instead of enhancing them. The first of these choices was her decision not to go to college, which closed off a wide range of options outside the film industry. Another choice she made early on was to stay in positions that paid well but were not otherwise very gratifying. Then, instead of planning an orderly transition into a different career, she just dropped out, which alienated many of her former co-workers and employers. When she went back to work, she chose a job that was even less fulfilling than her previous occupation.

In making these decisions Allison was reacting more to her parents and her own emotional state than to any actual failure on her own part. She had made some mistakes. She needed to adjust her expectations of success. She needed to develop her options, possibly by going back to school or training for a new occupation. But most of all Allison needed to realize that her past disappointments were caused not by fate or any lack of innate ability to succeed but by her own choices. She needed to accept responsibility for these choices and for the future decisions that would enable her to rebuild her life.

A SENSE OF MEANING

If you did not believe that you had any choices left or that the choices you made had any importance, you probably would stop taking responsibility for your choices. (Notice that I did not say that you would stop making choices. As long as you are alive and your mind is functioning, you are making choices.) You would become despondent and depressed. You would stop functioning normally. You might describe yourself as a victim or addict. You also might conclude that your life had no meaning.

While our feelings of self-efficacy come from the belief that we can succeed in a given situation, the deeper sense of meaning that we derive from our lives stems from the faith that we can somehow contribute in a positive way to the world around us. The difference between these two attitudes is largely a matter of degree, and yet it is not as if you can build up self-efficacy, like brownie points, to earn a sense of meaning. Self-efficacy and meaning continuously nourish each other. The minor miracles that we accomplish in our everyday lives contribute to our feeling that *all* of life is worth living, and our conviction that life has some overall purpose empowers us to keep attempting miracles.

Another way of describing meaning is usefulness. It is our sense of usefulness as well as efficacy that gives us pride and self-respect. It motivates us to help each other, to work at tasks that bring us no direct reward. It is the antidote to despair. In support of this idea, Viktor Frankl conducted a study of young patients who were suffering from depression as a result of being unemployed. Frankl persuaded the patients to become community volunteers, working with youth and adult education programs, public libraries, and other meaningful causes. Even though the patients remained unemployed, unpaid, and hungry, their depression lifted after they began volunteering. Frankl concluded, "Being jobless was equated with being useless, and being useless was equated with having a meaningless life."[6] By taking responsibility for their own choices and by directing those choices toward inherently worthwhile tasks, the patients rediscovered the meaning in their lives and began to heal themselves.

Choice, self-efficacy, usefulness, meaning. These are all irrelevant terms without the core component that ties them together: personal responsibility. If we do not take responsibility for our choices, we will always be at the uncertain mercy of whoever or whatever is directing us, and we will never feel the strength of our own minds. If we do not take responsibility for our actions, then we are not entitled to either the pleasure of success or the disappointment of failure that results from them. If we do not take responsibility for making the world slightly better for our existence, we will suffer our own uselessness. And if we do not take responsibility for finding and nurturing a sense of meaning, we will drift through life aimless and unfulfilled.

WHAT'S YOUR RESPONSIBILITY RATING?

How much responsibility are you willing to accept for your decisions and actions? If you aren't sure how to answer that question, the following exercise may help.

1. List your major life decisions. Think about the big decisions that have significantly affected the course of your life. If necessary, go all the way back to childhood and list such decisions as:

- Which friends or teachers would influence you
- Which schools you would attend
- What occupation(s) you would follow

- What religion you would follow
- Whether, when, and whom you would marry
- Where you would live
- Whether and when you would have children

Example:

In chronological order, Ted's major life decisions have included:

1. Becoming best friends with John Williams in tenth grade
2. Attending a state university
3. Going to Cornell Medical School
4. Becoming a doctor
5. Marrying Andrea
6. Going into private practice
7. Deciding to have children
8. Getting divorced

My **major life decisions** have been:

DECISIONS	RATING
1. _____	_____
2. _____	_____
3. _____	_____
4. _____	_____
5. _____	_____
6. _____	_____
7. _____	_____
8. _____	_____
9. _____	_____
10. _____	_____

TOTAL _____

OVERALL RESPONSIBILITY RATING (ratings total _____
divided by number of decisions)

2. Rate your responsibility for each of these decisions. Think about all the different people and factors that influenced each decision. Ask yourself whose choice it really was. Then rate your own responsibility on the following scale:

1 = I had no responsibility for the decision.
2 = I was slightly responsible.
3 = I was 50 percent responsible.
4 = I was mostly responsible.
5 = I was completely responsible.

Example:

Ted's parents had their hearts set on his becoming a doctor, and made tremendous sacrifices to make that possible. In retrospect, he felt that he never would have gotten through medical school if they hadn't pushed him so hard. If it had been up to him, he would have become a writer. On the other hand, he let them make the decision for him, so he was slightly responsible. Thus he gave himself a responsibility score of 2 for the decision to become a doctor.

3. Tally your individual ratings to come up with your overall responsibility rating. First, count the number of major life decisions on your list. Add up the responsibility ratings for all listings. Now divide your total by the number of listings. The result is your overall responsibility rating.

Rating	Interpretation
1 or 2	You tend to deny responsibility for your own decisions.
3 or 4	You try to share responsibility for your decisions.
5	You are willing to take full responsibility for your decisions.

The higher your rating, the more accurate your assessment of your personal responsibility is likely to be. Even if you were heavily influenced by other people or circumstances, you were in charge of your own decisions. Even if you did not think you had any alternative, you still had the choice between action or inaction. You were not powerless over your past decisions, and you are not powerless now.

If your rating was below 3, you may not have an accurate view of your past. It may help to go back through your life decisions and *claim* responsibility for them even if you don't *feel* responsible. Returning to our example, Ted did not feel that he had any responsibility at all for his divorce. His wife had fallen for another man. He had done everything he could to keep the marriage together, but she had left him anyway. Ted saw himself as his wife's victim. He needed to get out of this role if he was to pull his life back together. He needed to recognize that he shared responsibility for the marriage's breakup just as he shared responsibility for his other major life decisions. By claiming this responsibility up front, he began to see the ways in which he actually was responsible. He had neglected the marriage and the children while he was building his practice. He had suspected his wife's affair for months without confronting her. And he had walked out of marriage counseling after two weeks because he wanted to pretend that their marriage was perfect. Once Ted was able to acknowledge that each of these acts involved his personal choice, he began to accept his share of responsibility. And once he finally got his past into perspective, he was able to claim responsibility for his future.

NOTES

1. George Vaillant, *The Natural History of Alcoholism* (Cambridge, Mass.: Harvard University Press, 1983), p. 130.

2. Douglas Jehl, "Cocaine-Related Deaths Decline for First Time in a Decade, Federal Figures Reveal," *Los Angeles Times* (May 21, 1990): A17.

3. "Consumption of Hard Liquor in U.S. Reaches a 30-Year Low," *Los Angeles Times* (November 25, 1989): A2.

4. Larry Martz, "A Dirty Drug Secret," *Newsweek* (February 19, 1990): 74.

5. Viktor Frankl, *Man's Search for Meaning* (New York: Pocket Books, 1984), p. 86.

6. Frankl, p. 165.

CHAPTER 8

Focus on the Goal
Rather Than the Process of Recovery

Most self-help programs insist that recovery is a lifelong process: Because you have an incurable disease, you are forever recovering, never recovered, and even if you have been in remission for thirty years, you must still consider yourself sick, still attend group, still follow the program. This approach makes treatment a life sentence rather than an opportunity for renewal.

My approach to recovery is exactly the opposite. In my view, the vast majority of emotional and behavior problems are not diseases. Most of these problems can be completely resolved, but through self-reliance, not dependence on a particular program or group. The answer is not to submit to a lifetime of treatment, but to believe in recovery as an *attainable goal* and in your recovered self as an identity that you are ready and willing to embrace.

ARE YOU REALLY READY FOR CHANGE?

Complete recovery means change, and for many of us, change is threatening. Even change that will make us happier and healthier. Even life-saving change. Inertia and fear of the unknown dictate more of our choices than we would like to admit, but we have to get past these obstacles if we are to improve our lives.

Support and self-help groups combat inertia and fear by providing a safe environment in which members can begin the process of change, but few of these groups follow the process all the way through. Instead, the inertia that keeps a battered wife in an abusive marriage simply steps up a notch to keep her in her codependents' group, and the fear that originally kept her from seeking outside help now prevents her from trusting her own resources beyond the group. Self-help groups are like halfway houses. They serve a valuable function for many people, but they do not complete the process, and they often create an illusion of progress that may encourage backsliding. The case of John, in chapter 3, illustrates how this can occur. While he drew applause from his group as a model and leader, his destructive behavior actually worsened.

So how *do* you get past the inertia and fear of the unknown? The most important factor has nothing to do with the type of therapy, program, or group that you enlist to help you. It has to do with your willingness to relinquish your problems. During my years in practice I have seen intelligent, wealthy patients who appear to have everything going for them bounce from one form of counseling to another without making any progress because in the final analysis they are not willing to give up their chemical highs, their illusion of power, their sexual thrill-seeking or, quite simply, their preoccupation with their problems. On the other hand, I have seen many patients who had no special incentives or assistance but made up their minds to finally erase their problems from their lives and did so, largely on their own. The best examples of this phenomenon are people who smoke or eat too much or have lifetime habits such as nailbiting, who suddenly just get fed up and find whatever resources they need to quit their habits for good. Because so many of these people do not join groups or programs they are not generally included in statistical surveys, but we all can find numerous examples of these personal triumphs among our friends and neighbors.

In my work with substance abusers I've noticed that the abusers who are successfully rehabilitated generally fall into three distinct groups. The most likely to rehabilitate themselves are the men and women who, in their own minds, have hit bottom. Many have lost jobs, families, and homes and are so disgusted with themselves that they feel they literally have to choose between recovering and dying. Others have been in and out of treatment programs so many times that they become desperate to stop the cycle at any cost. As with the self-reformers described above, the problems finally lose so much of their appeal that the price of recovery is acceptable.

Other drug abusers with a good recovery rate have only recently started blacking out or receiving warnings from their families or employers, but, because of their values, they perceive these incidents as major crises, which creates the same cathartic effect as hitting bottom. This group includes people who may be physically addicted to drugs but still have a strong sense of identity that clashes with their role as addicts. It also includes people who have strong resources that they know will vanish if their drug use continues. This group ultimately values the rewards of a drug-free life enough that they are willing to sacrifice the rewards of addiction.

Finally, there are the abusers who use drugs for other purposes, including people with eating disorders who use cocaine and/or amphetamines to lose weight (which describes an estimated 50 to 70 percent of all people with eating disorders) and veterans who became addicted to heroin because it was readily available and "part of the scene" in Vietnam. These users didn't have a heavy emotional investment in drugs to begin with and usually can kick their habits relatively easily once they stop viewing themselves as addicts and begin to address their other, underlying problems.

Consider your own attitude toward your problems. The summary exercise at the end of chapter 4 gave you some objective criteria to measure the relative severity of your problems, but the decision to finally attack those problems is a purely subjective one. Nobody can make the decision for you or force you to make it against your will. For example, if the doctor tells you that your cholesterol is dangerously high, but you refuse to give up butter, eggs, and cream, then you're not likely to improve your cholesterol condition. It may take a heart attack to finally convince you that the pleasure of eating rich foods is not worth more than life itself. If you don't particularly care about food, however, you probably won't have any difficulty streamlining your diet. The doctor's message is the same, the prescription for recovery is the same; the key factor is your willingness to give up the goodies that are part of your problem.

Once you start to view your problems as an obstacle to life instead of a necessity of life, your drug, habit, or conflict will be less compelling than the promise of renewal. Your problem will no longer seem insurmountable. The goal of recovery will no longer seem impossible. And the prospect of change will no longer be so frightening.

UNCOVERING THE HIDDEN OBSTACLES TO RECOVERY

What if you *want* desperately to resolve your problems but still cannot believe that you are *capable* of complete recovery? Chances are that what's holding you back is not your capacity but your conception of recovery. You may have confused recovery with impossible dreams—becoming a billionaire, for example, or having the face and figure of someone half your age. Or you may be afraid to relinquish the problems. You might be getting more benefits from your injured or diseased identity than you realize. Alternatively, others may be pressuring you to stay as you are. It's important to sort out all these different factors.

Think of recovery as a business decision. Your life is a company in trouble. To save the business you may have to change its identity, reorganize the staff, eliminate nonproductive divisions, and experiment with new strategies to increase profits and restore the company to self-sufficiency. As the founder of this company, you have long resisted the idea of changing its identity. For all its problems, the firm is part of you; it was a source of pleasure as well as heartache, and it's always difficult to close the door on the past. But now that you recognize the need for change, you are surrounded by people inside and outside the company who oppose it. Those inside are afraid of losing their jobs or being reassigned. Some of your top officers have actually threatened to walk out on you if you go through with your recovery plan. Some outside observers are sabotaging your efforts because they fear that your reorganized firm will not honor its old contracts, while others suspect that the new, stronger firm will create unwelcome competition. So you have to make sure that you have enough support to carry the plan through and to weather the inevitable backlash. You also need to have a clear and realistic idea of the impact that your plan will have on the company: what it stands to gain, what it stands to lose, and whether the net result is in line with your recovery goals.

In your quest for personal recovery, you face the same identity conflicts as the company founder. The insiders who oppose you may include family members or close friends who, directly or indirectly, benefit from your problems. Your outside saboteurs may be friends, associates, or others who view your recovery as a threat.

Your plan for change, like the business owner's, must include clear, realistic goals that incorporate gains and losses, support and opposition. In short, you need to ask yourself the following questions:

What rewards do I get for *not* recovering? For one thing, you preserve your identity: how you have come to view yourself and how others view you. When you assume a new face, a new role in the universe, it is bound to create feelings of uncertainty and instability. So staying as you are, even with all your problems, can seem safer than adopting a new identity.

Certain problems can give you a way to rationalize unwanted behavior and feelings. For example, the recovering alcoholic who lies to his employer can blame his addiction for his deceit, and his wife may say that her codependence caused her to have an affair with a member of her self-help group. As we found in the last chapter, it is often easier to say that your problems have control of you than that you are responsible for them.

There may also be more tangible rewards. You might stay in an incompatible marriage, at least in part, because of the physical and financial security it gives you, or because you want to have a child, or because you have young children and want to be able to stay home with them. For substance abusers, the high of the drug is a very tangible reward. For anorexics, the loss of weight and the illusion of control are tangible rewards. And for many people in self-help programs, the attention, sympathy, and camaraderie of the group are powerful inducements to keep old problems alive. In these groups the *process* of recovery, the intense narcissistic focus on oneself, can be so intoxicating that it actually prevents the *attainment* of recovery.

Am I trying to protect or please someone by avoiding recovery? You may be avoiding recovery because someone else is pressuring you to stay as you are—or because you *think* someone else will be hurt or angered if you change. I see this most frequently among women in abusive marriages who are afraid that their husbands will come after them if they leave or who believe that their children are better in an intact family, even a violent one, than they will be if the family breaks up. Before these women can tackle their problems, they have to separate their own feelings about their situation from those of the other family members, and then they must ask themselves whom they are protecting and why.

Anyone who has a stake in your problems may inadvertently or intentionally prevent you from resolving them. This includes the leaders and sponsors in your self-help group who need you to identify yourself as weak and sick so that you will turn to them for help, become an advocate of the program, and recruit new members. However, they may not want you to recover completely, because then you would no longer need them or the group. You would also violate the model of addiction and victimization as incurable diseases. In the end, membership in a recovery group can be a lifetime imposition not because recovery requires a lifetime but because the group requires a growing membership.

Self-help groups can also lock you into your problems by imposing recovery goals that are unrealistic or ill suited to your particular needs. I have treated many AA/NA members, for example, who are so uncomfortable with the program's quasi-religious overtones that they "fail" because they will not submit to a Higher Power. Even if they quit using, the other members persuade them that they are really just "dry" until they admit their powerlessness and accept the terms of the program. Often, this rebuke triggers a relapse. Whatever treatment method or group you use, make sure that it is well suited to your particular needs and beliefs, or it may simply add new problems to the existing ones.

What do I stand to lose through recovery? For openers, you will lose your old injured identity, the sympathy and approval of those who have benefited from your problems, and your own preoccupation with your problems. You may also sacrifice some or all of the rewards associated with your old problems, though this might not be as painful as it seems. Many people who have conquered eating disorders find that food is less compelling after they have developed more constructive ways to assert control. Recovered substance abusers generally have a less exalted view of intoxication than they did when using. And lapsed Twelve Step followers often find that the solace and camaraderie of their old groups does not seem as meaningful in retrospect as it did when they were caught up in the program. The same forces that lured you into your problems or into the initial process of recovery may simply lose their power once you have fully recovered.

On the other hand, you may face some very real losses and perhaps even dangers in resolving your problems. Divorce, for example, is one of the most common means of resolving a troubled marriage, but it can have some unpleasant consequences. One spouse may lose contact with the children or suffer financial hardship. In some cases, there is the threat of physical violence.

It would be foolhardy to ignore such risks. The question that's always on the table, however, is whether they really outweigh the benefits of recovery. Which brings us to the next consideration.

What do I hope to gain through recovery? In this book, I use the word recovery to mean emotional and physical health, self-reliance, and stability. But the word has different meanings for different people. Before you can accurately evaluate your chances of recovery, you need to make sure that your own definition is realistic and honest.

At first glance it would seem that the object of recovery is simply to turn your problems around. If you can't sleep at night, you presumably would like to become a sound sleeper. If you are too heavy, you probably want to lose weight. If you no longer love your husband, you may be looking for a way to rejuvenate your marriage or else get out of it. But, given the layers of risks and rewards that surround most problems, resolution is not always the primary purpose of recovery.

Often, the driving motive is to gain revenge, victory, or control over people who cannot be conquered or controlled. In chapter 2, for example, Nina said she wanted to protect herself and her children from her husband's abusiveness, but her actual mission was to punish her husband, even at her children's expense. Nina viewed recovery not in terms of her own personal (I-oriented) accomplishments but in terms of other people's responses. Since her estranged husband would not capitulate, Nina could not recover. But when she adjusted her terms of recovery to focus on her own thoughts, feelings, and actions, her problems suddenly seemed manageable and she began to make real progress in dealing with them.

Another misconception is that recovery will eliminate *all* your problems. Patients often enter therapy in the hope that somehow, if they just understand themselves a little better, they will be able to make themselves thin, beautiful, rich, famous, powerful, and forever happy. But recovery is not an idyllic state of bliss. It is real life with coping mechanisms. It involves pleasure and pain, excitement and frustration, passion and tedium. It is the knowledge that each of these sensations is offset by others and that even if you could match J. Paul Getty's fortune or Meryl Streep's superstardom, you would not be free of problems. Recovery is the ability to meet these problems head on, resolve them as well as possible, and move ahead with your life.

IDENTIFY YOUR RECOVERY GOALS

This still leaves open the question of goals, those benchmarks that you must meet to reclaim your health and balance. I am not talking about programmed ideals, compulsory abstinence, or lifetime allegiance to a group, but about your own personal transformation. Your recovery goals are the personal changes and accomplishments that will lead you back to self-reliance.

Think about the ways in which each of your general problems affects your life. It may involve your emotions, your beliefs, and/or your behavior. Your recovery goals, then, will be to reverse these effects. As you will see when you set your own recovery goals at the end of this chapter, you may be able to identify several different behavioral, emotional, and belief goals for each problem.

As Sara's case illustrates, it is essential that your recovery goals *accurately* reflect your individual problems. Sara had used codeine and valium heavily for four years until she was twenty-three, when her mother sent her to a drug rehabilitation hospital for a month. She joined Narcotics Anonymous while still in the hospital and afterward continued going to meetings twice a week. When Sara first consulted me, she was twenty-five but looked considerably older. Thin and gaunt, she had dark circles beneath her eyes, and looked nervously around the room as she spoke. She had worked as a stock clerk and typist but had been unemployed for several months. And she recently had had a relapse, which she described as follows:

> I should never have accepted the first drink. I was having lunch with this executive who was considering me for a job as his assistant. He ordered a bottle of

wine and poured me a glass, and I felt kind of obligated to accept. But then instead of hiring me he put the make on me! I walked out on him, but afterward I felt so guilty and disgusted with myself for drinking that wine—I kept thinking how awful it would be to confess in group. I was going to have to start over anyway, so there just didn't seem any reason not to have a full-blown binge first. I looked up a guy I hadn't seen in years and scored. I was high for a week, until I ran out of money. Then I went back to group. It's like I'm an addict and there's nothing I can do about it. I'll always be an addict!

Sara had a number of serious problems, including her lack of a job, anxiety, and low self-worth, as well as her use of drugs. But the goals that her self-help group had set for her were a major problem in themselves.

I asked Sara if she enjoyed drinking. Not particularly, she told me. I asked if she had ever been drunk or gotten into trouble because of drinking. Never. In fact, the only drugs that Sara ever had used to excess were codeine and valium. She used them because they relieved her feelings of anxiety, and she specifically avoided many other drugs because they intensified her anxiety. Yet she had accepted NA's prescribed goal of total abstinence from all chemical substances without ever questioning whether it was appropriate for her particular problem. She had taken it so completely to heart that when she had this glass of wine she felt that she had failed, which heightened her anxiety and drove her right back to her drug of choice. It was not the alcohol that triggered her relapse but her confused view of recovery. She had been persuaded that the means equal the end, that the process of abstaining is the same as the goal of personal recovery. She needed to divorce herself from the process and reassess her goals.

The pattern of Sara's drug abuse began with fairly ordinary setbacks. An argument with her boyfriend, trouble at work or, as in this incident, a disappointing job interview would send her self-esteem plunging and her anxiety soaring. In the past, she had turned to drugs for relief. Now she used NA. But while the group offered moral support and reinforced her commitment to abstinence, it did not help her focus on the other major tasks in rebuilding her life.

Sara needed to develop skills and activities that would give her a sense of pride. She needed to find constructive ways to control her anxiety. She needed a more challenging job than the ones she'd had in the past. She needed to develop the assertiveness and confidence to face other people, including her self-help group, without allowing herself to be intimidated or controlled by them.

These were broad goals, which we would later refine to more specific ones, but they covered the basic sources of Sara's drug problem. They addressed her emotional, behavioral, and attitudinal needs. And they would give her a firm foundation for her new, self-reliant identity.

The lesson in Sara's story is that rigid, universal prescriptions simply don't work for everyone, and they can backfire disastrously. Unfortunately, the simple fact that AA's program is now touted as a "cure" for everything from using drugs to caring too much gives the impression that it *should* work for all of us and for everything that ails us. If and when it doesn't, the self-help and codependency movement leaders tell us, it's our fault for not following the program exactly. If we violate the program but achieve a sane, stable life by another route, they tell us we're in denial and have not really recovered because we didn't reach *their* prescribed goals along the way. It's worth asking whose goals they are, anyway? Who benefits from them? What good will come of them? If their purpose is simply to perpetuate the process of recovery, then they probably aren't worth pursuing. On the other hand, if the goals we set for ourselves will lead us through the process and on to the *ultimate* goal of a fully recovered, independent life, then we should embrace them.

SET YOUR RECOVERY GOALS

Setting clear goals is a vital part of recovery. To arrive at your recovery goals, review your list of general problems from chapter

4 (see page 83). Each problem may affect your emotions, behavior, and/or attitudes or beliefs. To identify your recovery goals, then, you need to reverse these effects.

Example: Jonas's general problem was that he gambled. This, of course, was a behavior in itself, so the primary recovery goal was to quit gambling. But it also had serious effects on other aspects of his behavior. Because of his gambling, he was not devoting enough attention to either his business or his family. And to conceal his losses, he had begun to lie to his wife and creditors. His gambling also was taking an emotional toll on him. Every time he won, his confidence soared, but his losses far outnumbered his wins, and with each loss he was filled with desperation and shame. He no longer believed in himself, in his own ability to succeed without the magic boost of a big win. And yet he believed that if he failed to succeed, he was worthless as a man. Jonas's recovery goals, then, were considerably more involved than simply quitting his gambling habit.

The following format helped Jonas to clarify his goals, and can work for you, too.

First, write out the general problem:

Example: *I gamble too much.*

_____

Now identify the most significant effects of the problem and reverse these effects to find your goals.

Behavioral effects:

Examples: *I'm not giving enough attention to my family.*
I lie to my wife and creditors.
I'm neglecting my business.

_____

_____

_____

Behavioral goals:

Examples: *Give my family the time and attention they deserve.*
Be honest with myself and others.
Get my business back on track.

_____

_____

_____

Emotional effects:

Examples: *I have no self-confidence unless I win.*
I feel desperate and ashamed whenever I lose.
I feel that I have no control over my life.

_____

_____

_____

Emotional goals:

Examples: *Restore my self-confidence.*
Learn to control my anxiety and feelings of shame.
Recover some sense of self-control.

_____

_____

_____

Attitudinal effects:

Examples: *I don't believe I can succeed on my own.*
I think I'm worthless unless I'm always winning.

_____

_____

_____

Attitudinal goals:

Examples: *Learn to believe in my own essential worth.*
Be able to accept and learn from failure.

_____

_____

_____

   Using this recovery roadmap, you can see where you're starting and where you hope to end. Now it's time to begin the
journey.

CHAPTER 9

Tackle Your Problems One at a Time

You have identified and prioritized your problems and targeted your recovery goals. Now you need to decide how you're going to achieve your goals.

The techniques that I recommend in this chapter do not require any Higher Power. They do not demand prayer or humility, and will not ask you to proselytize or carry any message of spiritual awakening to other people with problems. I do not pretend that these techniques are a panacea. *They* are not the solutions to your problems, but they will give you a format and method to find and implement those solutions. Using this guiding structure, you can change your life.

BASIC PROBLEM-SOLVING STRATEGY

Psychologists use a wide range of problem-solving techniques. This particular strategy is one I have devised in my own practice. I have used it myself and have seen it work for my patients and patients of the hundreds of therapists I have supervised over the years. It works because it guides you to solutions that are both feasible and appropriate for your particular needs, and because it puts you in control. It prompts you to take possession of both your problems and their solutions. In the process, you realize a sense of mastery rather than dependence. You gain the confidence and the tools you need, not just to solve one problem, but to reclaim your life.

Here, then, is an overview of the process.

1. Focus on one problem at a time.
2. Identify your specific goals.
3. Brainstorm possible solutions.
4. Evaluate each solution.
5. Select one solution and one contingency solution.
6. Reevaluate the problem.
7. Develop your plan.
8. Guard against self-sabotage.
9. Implement your plan and monitor your progress.
10. Plan to prevent recurrence of the original problem.

Now let's look at each of these steps in detail. At the end of this chapter you will find a worksheet to help you apply this process to your own problems.

1. Focus on One Problem at a Time

You have already done the groundwork for this step. You've identified and prioritized your general problems and broken down the most urgent ones into specific problems. Now you need to target just one specific problem for resolution.

Start with the general problem that tops your priority list. Then look at all related specific problems and choose one to address first. It may be the one that is causing you the most immediate distress, such as the migraine headache that makes it impossible for you to think about anything else. It may be one that has a deadline, such as the rent you must pay by the end of the month. Or it may be the problem you can resolve the most quickly and easily, such as organizing the family to do more of the household chores each day. Whichever you choose, the important thing is to give it your full attention. Try to put all your other worries out of your mind for the moment, and pretend that this is your only problem.

At first, this may cause you some anxiety. If you're accustomed to juggling multiple crises, you may be convinced that they'll all come toppling down if you stop to deal with just one. You delude yourself that if you keep juggling long enough, the crises will play themselves out. Meanwhile, you remain enslaved by your problems, and nothing ever gets resolved. You cannot deal effectively with more than one conflict at a time, and that means that you may have to put some matters on hold while you focus on your top priority. Some of the other problems may temporarily worsen while your attention is elsewhere, but the strength and confidence you gain by resolving this first conflict will enable you, in turn, to deal more effectively with the others.

2. Identify Your Specific Goals

In the last chapter you identified your general recovery goals. When you reach these goals, you will know that your general problems are resolved. Now, since you're dealing with one specific problem, you need to target the changes or achievements that will signify this problem's resolution.

In identifying these goals you need to follow the same criteria that you used to define your problem. That is, your goals must:

- Be attainable. (If you are terrified of speaking in public, your initial target might be to address a group of five or six people but not a packed auditorium.)
- Include clear and concrete terms for success. (If you suffer from depression, "happiness" is too vague to be a useful goal, but "returning to a normal eight-hour sleep schedule" is clear and concrete.)
- Focus on things you can do to better your life now, not things you should have done differently in the past or hope to do differently in years to come. (If you are struggling to

reconstruct your life after a divorce, your goal is to support yourself and develop new social relationships, not to figure out how you might have saved the marriage.)

- Reflect your existing resources, abilities, and character. (If you have a violent temper, look for ways to control or divert your anger, but don't expect to eliminate it.)
- Exclude ambitions over which you have little or no control. (You cannot count on winning the lottery, eliminating sexism or racism, or finding a miracle cure for aging. You can, however, improve the quality of your personal relationships, develop new skills to secure a higher-paying job, become more involved in your community, and take better care of your physical health.)
- Be "I-oriented" and thus exclude goals that depend on other people's reactions. (If you've been through an ugly custody battle, you need to repair and strengthen your own relationship with your children, not destroy their relationship with your former spouse.)
- Reflect something that *you* really want to achieve, not something you're doing solely because you think you're supposed to or because someone else is pressuring you. (If you have decided to lose ten pounds to please your husband but you don't really want to lose the weight, you're probably not going to lose the weight.)

It is also important to consider the totality of your life, including how you think and behave, and what you feel and believe. If your goals are too limited, you may achieve them without seeing any significant or enduring change in the underlying problems. When researchers asked a group of ninety relapsed alcoholics to describe what they had to do to recover, 34 percent said they had to abstain from alcohol and 29 percent said they just had to attend AA meetings. Indeed, on average they had attended 586 AA or NA meetings apiece![1] Yet they kept relapsing. One reason, concluded the researchers, was that their recovery goals were too narrow. They did not consider self-awareness to be an important goal, for example. Nor did they associate recovery with success in relationships, or with acquiring coping skills or a sense of purpose in life. In short, they failed to repair the underlying causes of their addiction, and so left themselves open to relapse.

3. Brainstorm Possible Solutions

Imagine that you are looking at a maze. The starting point is your problem. Your goals are the end point. Each path in the maze is a possible solution, a potential route from your problem to your goals. Before you can solve the maze, you need to survey all of these paths. You need to scan your options.

Now try to envision all possible approaches to your real goals. Opening your mind and using your imagination are the two most important keys here. Relax and let your thoughts wander. Jot down every idea and keep on thinking. Collect as many different possibilities as you can.

If you are having difficulty, try the following techniques:

Think crazy. Perhaps the most important point to remember when brainstorming is to reach for solutions that seem absurd or impossible. For example, if your problem is that you fly into a rage whenever your son misbehaves, it might well cross your mind that locking him in his room or sending him to live with his grandmother would solve your problem. Your natural tendency may be to push these notions aside because they make you feel guilty or because you know that you would never consider actually following through with them. Yet it is important to list them alongside your other, more obvious and rational ideas, such as controlling your own temper. Later, when you step back and survey your list, you may find unexpected information in those crazy ideas. They may suggest that you need to take a break from your child or that you need some outside help in dealing with him. Remember, sometimes when you feel that you're being irrational, you are really just being honest, and it's always a mistake to discount those honest responses.

Work backward. Imagine that you've attained your goal. Now, inch your way backward. Ask yourself what was the last thing you did before achieving the goal. Continuing with the example from above, imagine that your child has just thrown a temper tantrum and you've calmly gotten him through it. That's your end goal. Now, move the scene back a notch, and try to imagine what you would have said to him while he was screaming. Would you have remained silent? Would you have tried to get him to talk through his feelings? Would you have tried to quiet him by singing to him? Jot all these possibilities down, then move back another frame to see how you might have reacted when the tantrum started. Would you have counted to ten? Would you have left the room to collect yourself? Would you have quietly restrained your child in your arms? Make a note of all these possible reactions, and work all the way back to the start of the incident that precipitated the tantrum. When you finish, you will find that your notes provide a variety of possible solutions to the problem of dealing with your child's behavior.

Ask for suggestions. Many self-help groups and therapists discourage personal advice giving. While they may stress general principles or program philosophy, they tend to resist suggestions based on personal experience or insight. In some cases this is because the program is supposed to be all-encompassing and all things to all people, and to offer more specific advice would run the risk of contradicting the program. In other cases, it's because the therapist or group feels obliged to be unconditionally supportive, and to give advice would run the risk of challenging or offending the individual. Whatever the reason, I believe that such restraint is counterproductive. Other people can be a vital source of ideas and possibilities. Of course, not all of the advice you receive will be good or appropriate for your particular needs, but it may prompt you to consider directions or opportunities that you otherwise would have ignored. By discussing your problem with other people and asking how they would handle it, you not only will gather some possible answers, but you may also elicit much-needed support. If you feel that your problem is too private to reveal, you can still get help by discussing it indirectly. For example, if you've discovered that your husband is having an affair, you may not want to publicize this fact, but you can certainly explore the issue of infidelity in general terms and ask your friends what they would do if they discovered that their husbands had cheated on them. Remember, considering a piece of advice does not obligate you to follow it. The value of seeking outside suggestions is simply that it opens your eyes to a wider array of options than you can generate on your own.

Research the problem. Spend an afternoon at the library investigating your problem. Look for help not only from self-help books and magazine articles but from novels and biographies about people in situations similar to yours. If you drink too much—or think you do—become an expert on the diagnosis and treatment of alcoholism. If your mother has recently died and you cannot seem to recover, look for suggestions from authors who have experienced or studied the grieving process. As with personal advice from friends, you may find that you disagree with some of what you read, but take down the suggestions anyway. The better informed you are and the more options you can identify, the more power you wield over your problem. One caution here, however. It is possible to go overboard with this advice and spend so much energy on the research that you lose sight of your own problem. Try to keep your personal situation firmly in mind as you gather your information, and remember that you are looking for realistic *solutions*, not just reams of background material.

4. Evaluate Each Solution

Once you have a wide range of solutions to choose from, you will need to decide which are the most feasible and the most likely to lead you to your goals. You may be tempted to scratch certain ideas off the list because they seem ridiculous or impossible, but if you pull back and look at them more objectively you may discover that they're not as far off base as you thought. Likewise, the solutions that seem the most appealing, or that others recommend most highly, may prove to be inappropriate in your particular circumstances. For these reasons, it's a good idea to subject even the most unlikely options to the following list of questions.

Do I believe that this solution can work for me? If you have no faith that a particular plan will work, you won't put enough effort into it to make it work. That, in effect, will sabotage it. If you don't believe in it, don't want to believe in it, and can't make yourself believe in it, you need a different solution.

Is this solution suited to my personality? By personality, I mean the basic character traits that you cannot and do not want to change in yourself—for example, whether you are gregarious or introverted, quiet or talkative, slow- or fast-paced, cautious or eager. If your plan of action demands a different type of personality, then you are not likely to succeed. Perhaps your problem is that you tend to freeze up on your first date with a new person. One possible solution is to substitute group activities for one-on-one dates. This way, less attention is focused solely on you, and there will be other conversation to cover the awkward gaps when you can find nothing to say. But this will work only if you are, in fact, more relaxed in group settings than you are with one person. If you tend to withdraw in groups, or if you are likely to worry that others in the group may "steal" your date, then you probably will need to find a different tactic, such as equipping yourself with jokes to break the ice, or requesting that you and your date go to a favorite place where you will feel more at ease.

Is this solution suited to my personal values and beliefs? Twelve Step programs, like religions, are most beneficial for people who come to the program with a basic belief in God and the value of spiritual surrender and redemption. As we've already discussed, people who do not have any spiritual faith in God, who embrace an existential philosophy of life, tend to balk at the Twelve Steps' religious and moralistic overtones, and frequently "fail" in observing the programs. While Twelve Step leaders generally would say that these individuals should adjust their values and beliefs to conform to the program, I have found that the most effective therapies, even for hard-core addictions to drugs and alcohol, work with the individual's values to produce workable, realistic solutions. What does this mean for you? It means that you need to examine your own attitudes—what makes you happy, what puts you at ease, what gives you pride and satisfaction, what you want out of life. For example, if you are recovering from an abusive relationship, ask yourself what you want out of love, what matters most to you in an intimate relationship. If love, for you, hinges on mutual need and desire, then you will have a hard time embracing the "detached" ideal proposed by most codependency programs. Maybe you need to adjust your selection process so that you end up with partners who share your values. Maybe you need to change the ground rules going into your next relationship so that you don't become involved too quickly, before you really know your partner. But if your solution is predicated on fettering your emotions or completely redefining your basic personal values, then you probably won't be satisfied with the resulting relationships. You may achieve the goals that the codependency movement sets for you, but it's doubtful that you'll achieve your *own* goals.

Do I have or can I obtain the resources I need to make this solution work? These may include time, money, information, family or social support, special talents or skills. If you hate your job, then a career change may be one possible answer to your problem. As you assess other job opportunities, however, you must ask yourself what resources each one will require. Will you need retraining or further education? Will it require a personal financial investment? Will your family approve of this new occupation? Do you have enough information about this new business to make a success of it? If you don't have the necessary resources, can you obtain them? The object is not to discourage yourself but to plan for potential hazards and obstacles. If you cannot come up with any way around an obstacle—if, for example, you are thinking of becoming a doctor but are already forty years old and cannot afford the time or the money it would require to go through medical school—then you may have to select a different course of action.

When you have reviewed all possible solutions, identify the ones that most closely fit the above criteria. Your best solutions will be those that promise the most advantages and least disadvantages.

5. Select One Solution and One Contingency Solution

After you have evaluated all the possible solutions, give yourself some time to mull them over. Try to step back from the problem and stop thinking about it for a day or two. Sometimes when your mind is on something completely different you will experience a flash of insight or recognition that will help you decide how to act. And even if you don't have any special revelation, you will return to the selection process with a fresh perspective. At that point, identify the two solutions that seem most practical and appropriate.

Your first choice should be one that has passed all your evaluating criteria. It must be one to which you are willing to commit; however, this does not mean that you are necessarily eager to try it or confident of your ability to succeed, or that you feel comfortable with it. If you had a malignant growth on your leg, you would probably choose to have it surgically removed, but that does not mean that you would look forward to the operation or feel comfortable about it, or even that you would have much faith that it would actually stop the cancer. You would elect to have the surgery because it promised the most long-term benefits and the least disadvantages of all your options.

Of course, even if you faithfully follow your planned solution, it might not work as well as expected. For this reason, you need your second choice as a backup plan. Perhaps you have decided that the best way to stop your parents from interfering in your life is to reason with them, sit them down and explain that while you appreciate their concern, you are a grown person and would prefer to make your own decisions. However carefully you control the time, place, and tone of your meeting, your parents still may refuse to heed your request. You may need a harder-hitting approach. Your contingency, then, might be to stop discussing any pending decisions with your parents.

6. Reevaluate the Problem

Imagine that you are hiking over a mountain from one valley to another. You've dreamed of making this journey, and now you are at the top of the mountain. Looking back, you can see the village where you started. On either side, you can see higher mountains, plains, and other valleys. Ahead, for the first time, you can actually survey your destination. Based on what you see, you may decide to go forward as planned, or you may decide that this valley doesn't look so promising, after all, and strike out in a different direction. As you calculate the additional time and energy it will take to complete the journey, you may also decide that the hike itself isn't as rewarding as you expected, in which case you may turn back home to spend the rest of your day on another activity entirely.

In much the same way, many of my patients reach this point in solving their problems only to discover that they've been attacking the wrong problems or aiming for the wrong goals. Although they have not yet solved their problems, they are close enough that they can now envision resolution, and can see whether it will bring them the relief they had anticipated. The results are sometimes surprising.

Years ago I was supervising a therapist whose patient, Jerome, was planning to get a divorce. Jerome was extremely unhappy and frustrated by his inability to please his wife. He believed that the marriage was doomed and, after evaluating all of his options, concluded that divorce would solve his problem. So the therapist asked Jerome to imagine that he had his divorce, that the marriage was finished and he no longer had anything to do with his wife. How did he feel now? Jerome had to admit that a divorce would probably have no significant effect on his unhappiness. In fact, he eventually realized that his marriage was not the real problem at all, but a smoke screen for the confusion and fear that had surrounded Jerome after his twin brother's recent death. Unable to come to terms with the death or even reveal his feelings, Jerome had convinced himself that the only way to protect himself was to cut himself off from everyone close to him. This drastic action was a distraction and a defense against his deeper conflict, but it would not resolve that conflict and, he finally saw, it would leave him more frightened and alienated, not less. What he needed was not to divorce his wife but to start the process over and, with her support, develop the tools to cope with his grief.

At this stage in the process, you may discover that your original, or presenting, problem is not the one you really need to solve, in which case you would start over with the newly identified problem, or you may decide that you would rather stay as you are than make the required changes. More likely, however, you will reaffirm your desire to work through your original problem and move ahead to the next step.

7. Develop Your Plan

What will it take to execute your solution? What exactly do you need to do? When will you do it? How will you do it? Will you need help? What is the order of action? The more detailed and organized your plan is, the greater your chances will be of succeeding.

Maryanne decided that the solution to her anxiety at work was to confront her boss about the promotions that he had repeatedly awarded to candidates whom Maryanne considered to be less qualified than herself. If she discovered that there was a valid reason for the bypasses, she would know what she needed to do to measure up. If she discovered that her boss was playing favorites, she might have to change jobs, but at least she would stop feeling as though she were crazy. Either way, she believed, her anxiety would diminish. But the inquiry had to be handled delicately, or she might alienate her boss unnecessarily or fail to get the information she needed. After careful consideration, Maryanne mapped out the following plan:

1. Carefully research the situation and gather all the facts beforehand.
2. Rehearse the conversation and get feedback from a close friend, preferably someone who knows how the boss is likely to react.
3. Select a day and time when the boss is not rushed or distracted by other urgent business.
4. Make an appointment, leaving adequate time.
5. Be prompt and businesslike at the meeting.
6. Pace the conversation, allowing time for the boss to answer each question without feeling pressured.
7. Make sure that the boss understands my position.
8. Based on the outcome of the meeting, decide whether to stay in this position or look for a new job.

Maryanne felt a little silly drawing up this plan. It seemed very simplistic. Yet the act of thinking it through and writing it out helped her clarify exactly what was required. It decreased the ambiguity of her situation, and as a result decreased her anxiety. When she reviewed the plan, it seemed very concrete and feasible. And when she felt the anxiety rising in her throat as she stood outside the boss's door, she was able to calm herself by reviewing the plan in her mind and focusing on the last step, which would finally resolve the dilemma that had been dogging her for years.

When we struggle with a difficult problem we all have a tendency to regress a little. When we're very angry or hurt or anxious, we tend to act "like a child." And, like children, we cope best in these situations when we have a clearly defined structure within which to work. The framework may seem obvious or simplistic, but it helps us to focus and act in a responsible way. It increases our chances of success.

8. Guard Against Self-Sabotage

Every time we attempt a major change in our lives, there is a part of us that resists, holding back or actively sabotaging the change. That resistant impulse can push an abused woman back into the arms of her violent husband even after she's safely divorced. It can prompt a smoker to suddenly reach for a cigarette after two weeks without a single puff. It can trigger an eating binge in someone who has been aggressively dieting for two months. The impulse is natural and normal, but you are not at its mercy. If you anticipate and plan for it, you can override it.

The more control you allow yourself in solving your problem, the more carefully you must plan for backsliding. Alcoholics who rely on AA to keep them sober generally do not plan for self-sabotage. They rely on the group's surveillance and on the rigid requirement of abstinence to provide the external controls that they lack within themselves. This is one reason why so few AA members are able to break free of the program. Those who have been addicted to alcohol who successfully moderate their drinking, however, establish different kinds of controls. Most realize that willpower alone is not enough. They generally set very specific limits on their drinking and impose certain rules and devices to help themselves stay within those limits. Some allow themselves only one drink within a certain time period. Others permit themselves to drink only at a certain hour or on certain days or with other moderate drinkers. Still others ritualize their drinking as part of meals, and drink only with their families.

Such controls may seem artificial, but they are not really any more contrived than the basic lifestyle rules that most of us take for granted. We sleep and eat at certain hours. We eat different foods for breakfast than for dinner. We dress and behave casually in some situations, formally in others. We use one style of language to talk to our family and close friends, another in addressing authority figures. And we set countless deadlines for ourselves to accomplish the tasks that fill our days. Viewed objectively, all these schedules and dress and behavior codes may seem pointless, but they give our lives a sense of order, discipline, and regularity. They help us organize our thoughts and behavior, and ironically, by measuring up to these otherwise arbitrary expectations, we heighten the sense that we are in control of our lives rather than the other way around.

9. Implement Your Plan and Monitor Your Progress

Finally, the moment comes when you must turn your solution into action. Ideally, the process of planning will have allayed some of the anxiety that you may be feeling, and the prospect of success will outweigh the fear of failure. But it's still possible that residual or peripheral feelings of pain or anger may get in your way. This frequently happens in cases where someone has been wronged and the solution is to separate from the perpetrator, but the anger is so intense that the victim cannot break free. One of my patients, Kate, spent four months evaluating all the possible ways in which she could resolve the pain caused by her husband's infidelity, and she finally decided that divorce was the best solution. She made a detailed plan to guide her through the divorce process, but when the time came to implement the plan, her anger held her back. If she broke away from her husband and received the settlement that he had already promised to pay, she would have no immediate target for her rage. Kate had to decide at this point whether she was capable of putting her anger aside and releasing herself from the marriage, or whether she needed to stop and deal with her anger as a separate problem in itself.

It can be extremely difficult to stop thinking about your problem and take the action that will resolve it. It may help to remind yourself that few serious problems, especially ones that have gone on a long time, ever go away on their own. They may get worse or spawn other problems so that they become unrecognizable, but they will not simply evaporate.

It may also help to realize that the benefits of solving a given problem are often as complex as the problem itself. When you heal one aspect of your life it is bound to affect your other relationships, performance, and feelings. These changes may be predictable or so subtle that you don't even realize they're connected to the problem. After Kate finally went ahead with her divorce, she found that she was much closer to her two young daughters and also a much better disciplinarian than she had been. She also was able to talk to her mother for the first time in ten years. And in a matter of weeks her anger toward her husband had diminished to such an extent that, to her surprise, she realized that she was the stronger and saner of the two of them; her anger had given way to a new sense of strength and confidence.

To make sure that your solution is working as planned, check your progress periodically. Don't expect your problem to vanish overnight, and don't be discouraged if others crop up in its place. But if you're moving forward, you should be able to answer "yes" to each of the following questions:

- Is the original problem abating?
- Do I spend less time thinking about the problem?
- Is the problem causing me less discomfort?
- Do I feel that my life is changing?
- Am I satisfied with the pace of change?
- Are the changes causing more positive than negative effects in other areas of my life?

If, after several weeks of implementing your solution, you are not progressing in these areas, go back to Step 5 and set your contingency plan in motion. If none of your solutions seem to work, turn to the next chapter. You may need professional help.

10. Plan to Prevent Recurrence of the Original Problem

We all have a tendency to repeat old mistakes and fall back into negative patterns. That doesn't make us victims, it just means we're human.

The danger is that after you've solved one specific problem you may believe that you have the wider problem licked. And then, when you're confronted with exactly the same circumstances that led to the initial problem, you walk right into it again. You need to identify the patterns of behavior that have gotten you into trouble in the past and develop special strategies to change those patterns.

I worked with Linda for nearly a year before she was able to extricate herself from a painful, long-standing affair with a married man who worked in her office. She had finally broken off the relationship and gotten her life back to normal. She had a new job, was feeling proud of herself, and had promised herself that her next serious relationship would be solid and committed. She wanted to get married and have children, not to get ensnared in another illicit affair. Yet Linda had never experienced a stable relationship. She had been involved with three married men who had refused to leave their wives for her, and two single men who had refused to contemplate marriage. If she was ever to reach her goal, she would have to understand the pattern of her past behavior and develop a plan for changing it.

To help Linda clarify her pattern, I asked her to make a list of all the men she had met at her new job. Then I asked her to rank them, from the ones who most attracted her romantically to the ones who least attracted her. Next, she was to identify each man's positive and negative traits, as she saw them. Linda quickly realized that of the twenty men on her list the ones who most attracted her also aroused the most ambivalence in her. On the positive side, she found them to be good-looking, well-dressed, well-spoken, highly energetic, and generally charismatic. Most of them occupied positions of authority, or at least superiority, over Linda. On the negative side, she disliked their flirtatiousness. Most were reputed to have had affairs with other women in the office, and several were married. Linda did not trust most of these men, and she suspected some of them of unethical business practices.

Initially, Linda assumed that she was blinded by the men's good looks and power, but when she looked at the full list she realized that there were several others in the office whom she had not targeted who were equally handsome and in even higher positions. Then Linda realized that it was actually the flirtatious men's *negative* traits that were pulling her in. On the one hand, she saw them as challenges. Deep down, she thought that if she could just get close enough to them, she could change them. On the other hand, she was both impressed and daunted by their come-ons. She did not feel strong enough to reject their advances.

I asked Linda to think about the man she had ranked as most attractive, and imagine that he was taking her out. Based on her past experience with similar men, we rehearsed what was most likely to happen. We explored how she would feel when he pressured her to sleep with him, when he got up and went home to his wife, when he ignored her the next day at work, when he cut off the relationship and told her he could never marry her.

This scenario was Linda's best defense against repeating her past mistakes. Now that she'd identified the general type of men who were likely to cause her the most difficulty, her guard went up whenever she was around them. If they flirted or made advances, she would replay the scenario in her mind, and it provided the strength she needed to dismiss their advances.

The other part of her defense plan was to give more careful consideration to the kinds of men she'd always dismissed in the past. Should she really have to conquer someone to persuade him to marry her? Did she really need this kind of challenge in her love life, or would she be happier with someone who shared her goals from the start? What was wrong with a man who was moderately good-looking and genuinely kind and loving? Linda needed to break her old habits and adjust her expectations. It took time, and it wasn't easy, but she knew that if she didn't make these changes she'd probably be stuck in unsatisfactory relationships for the rest of her life.

Here, in a nutshell, is the strategy that enabled Linda to change her negative pattern:

- Identify your past mistakes and why you made them.
- Survey your current life for enticements to repeat those mistakes.
- Imagine that you went ahead and made the mistakes over again, and look at the consequences awaiting you.
- Remember those consequences whenever you are tempted to fall back into your old behavior patterns.
- Look at the healthy alternative behaviors that will steer you away from your old problems.
- Turn these alternatives into a new behavior pattern.

IF NECESSARY, GET HELP

Ideally, this strategy, like the others in this book, will help you to overcome your problems on your own. Some situations, however, are difficult or even impossible to resolve without outside help and support. If, after all the suggestions made thus far, you feel that you cannot deal with your conflicts alone, then you may need professional guidance. The next chapter will provide information to help you select the most appropriate treatment for your particular problem.

DESIGN YOUR OWN SOLUTION

Use this worksheet to apply the strategy you've just learned to your own problems.

1. Focus on one problem at a time.

Identify your general problem: _____

Identify the related specific problems: _____

_____

_____

_____

_____

Target one specific problem to resolve now:

_____

(If you are having difficulty, go back and review chapter 4, "Define Your Problems Without Labeling Yourself.")

2. Identify your specific goals.

Describe the changes or achievements that will mark the resolution of your target problem. For example, Laura, a young mother who feels trapped at home taking care of her young children, might set goals that include spending more time socializing with friends or getting a job outside the home.

Your goals: _____

_____

_____

3. Brainstorm possible solutions.

Jot down as many possible ways to achieve your goals as you can imagine. The possible solutions for Laura might include hiring a regular babysitter, asking her parents to spend more time looking after the children, leaving the children with her husband to take a class one or two evenings a week, taking a job with a company that provides on-site childcare, or socializing more with other young mothers and their children. Remember, for the moment you need not worry whether the solutions are feasible or desirable. Just collect as many options as you can.

_____

_____

_____

_____

4. Evaluate each solution.

Use the following checklist to evaluate each of your solutions:

- I believe that this solution could work for me.
- This solution is well suited to my personality.
- This solution is well suited to my personal values and beliefs.
- I have the resources I need to make this solution work.

Now list the solutions that fit all of the statements above.

_____

_____

_____

5. Select one solution and one contingency solution.

From the qualifying solutions you've just identified, choose one to try.

_____

In case that solution does not work, choose one contingency.

_____

  Example: Laura's primary solution might be to socialize more with other mothers, but she may find that she needs a different kind of stimulation. Her backup solution may be to enroll in a class.

6. Reevaluate the problem.

Imagine that you have followed through with your solution and your original problem is resolved. Now, with this image in mind, ask yourself the following questions:

- Was this the problem I really needed to solve?
- Has solving this problem brought the rewards that I expected?
- Was solving this problem really worth the investment of time, money, and energy that it required?

If you answer no to these three questions, stop here and reevaluate your original problem and goal. If you conclude that achieving your goals will not bring the desired results or that this problem does not really warrant any further attention, return to the beginning of the worksheet and begin the process over by targeting a different problem and a different set of goals.

7. Develop your plan.

Describe in order precisely what you must do to implement your solution. Include decisions that must be made and information that must be gathered as well as the specific actions that you must take to solve your problem. Also set a deadline by which you must either be making significant progress toward your goal or else will change to a different solution.

_____

_____

_____

_____

_____

_____

_____

_____

_____

Example: To develop new social relationships, Laura charted the following plan:

1. Look into children's classes at the local YMCA or public parks where it's possible to meet other parents.
2. Sign up for one or two of these classes.
3. Talk to the other parents in the class about doing other activities with the children.
4. Identify one or two other parents who seem interested in developing a friendship.
5. Plan a special outing, perhaps to the museum, with these other families.

6. Arrange a day each week to spend with these new friends.
7. If no significant friendships have evolved after two months, or if the time spent with these people is not satisfying or stimulating, enroll in a literature class at night.

8. Guard against self-sabotage.

Think of all the ways in which you might thwart your plan. Write them down and, alongside, write one or two suggestions to prevent yourself from sabotaging your plan.

Sabotage: **Prevention:**

_____   _____

_____   _____

_____   _____

_____   _____

_____

Example: Laura is very timid in strange situations and has difficulty making small talk. To force herself to connect with other mothers she decided to volunteer as an assistant in one of the baby classes she was attending with her daughter. She also made a point of having conversations with at least two people in each class. Recognizing the ways in which she typically avoids discussion, she specifically forbade herself to stand in the corner or focus solely on her children.

9. Implement your plan and monitor your progress.

Put your solution into action. Check your progress at specific intervals. Note your accomplishments and setbacks as well as the status of the original problem.

Progress/Change:

Week ____: _____

Week ____: _____

Week ____ : _____

Week ____ : _____

Week ____ : _____

Week ____ (Deadline for change): _____

Here is Laura's weekly progress report:

Week 1: Signed up for two classes at the Y and attended the first one.

Week 2: Volunteered to assist the teacher in baby gym class, made plans to go to the park Monday with Mary and Jane and their children.

Week 3: Met four more people in class and went to both the park and the museum with Mary and Jane.

Week 4: Had several of the women and kids from class over for lunch. The house seems a lot less claustrophobic with company!

Week 5: Accepted a job teaching one of the baby classes at the Y, and met some of the other staff members.

Week 6 (Deadline for change): The original problem is solved. I'm out of the house. I can bring the kids to the Y and still meet other adults. It may not be a permanent solution, but I no longer feel trapped.

10. Plan to prevent recurrence of the original problem.

Look at the circumstances that contributed to your original problem. Try to identify any patterns or influences that might recur. Identify ways that you can avoid or overcome these recurrences.

Negative pattern/Influence: **Deterrent:**

_____   _____

_____   _____

_____   _____

Example: Looking back to the time when she had felt so lonely and restricted, Laura saw three major contributing factors—and potential antidotes that would prevent each one from recurring. One was that she had recently moved and did not know anyone in the neighborhood; if she moved again, she decided, she would immediately join a school organization or community center where she could meet other parents. Another factor in her past unhappiness was that she had looked to her husband, who worked very long hours, for all her social stimulation; from now on she would see to it that she had several women friends who were available to her even when her husband was not. And a third was that she had been so involved with her children that she had repressed her own social needs; Laura now realized that there were ways to dovetail her children's and her own needs, that they were not mutually exclusive.

NOTES

1. Emil Chiauzzi, "Breaking the Patterns That Lead to Relapse," *Psychology Today* (December 1989): 18–19.

CHAPTER 10

Select a Treatment Program That Nurtures Self-Reliance, Not Dependency

I hope that the strategies and techniques described in this book are helping you to resolve your problems. However, no book can provide all the answers, and not everyone can easily apply written suggestions to real life. If you have tried these techniques and they just don't seem to be working, there are several possible reasons:

- You may not see your problems clearly enough to conquer them on your own.
- You may not be able to generate or implement the appropriate solutions.
- You may think you've solved the problem, but it keeps recurring.
- You may suffer not from tangible problems but from "bad feelings"—depression, anxiety, obsessiveness—which may be caused by biochemical imbalances or physical illness.
- Your problem may have existed for so long that your whole life revolves around it.
- You may have experienced a traumatic event and not know how to gauge or manage your reactions.

In short, you may need professional therapy or counseling.

Fortunately, the stigma once attached to psychotherapy and related treatments has diminished. The willingness to get help in times of crisis is now recognized as a strength rather than a weakness. The question is no longer whether to seek therapy but which of the many different therapeutic approaches is most appropriate for your particular problem.

As with any service, it's important to shop selectively for the mental health treatment that meets your specific needs. This is not easy when you are in a crisis frame of mind, but try to remember that the therapy you choose may make the difference between continued distress and full recovery.

In general, the most effective therapists and programs do *not* restrict themselves to single issues, do *not* stereotype individuals, and do *not* confuse God with self-control or use therapy to project blame. Successful treatment programs do not function as religions or weapons. Rather, they focus on the total person and use therapy to move beyond blame to self-reliance. But before starting any treatment program it's important to clarify what you expect from therapy and what the different types of treatment offer.

THE PURPOSE OF TREATMENT

Psychotherapy, counseling, medication, behavioral treatments, and support and self-help groups each can serve an important purpose. That purpose is to help you through a difficult period and foster constructive change. It is not to prop you up for the rest of your life.

I realize that this is exactly the opposite of the advice doled out by Twelve Step advocates. Melody Beattie, for example, writes, "If you used to go to meetings but stopped going, go back. If you start going, go for the rest of your life. Alcoholism is a lifetime illness that requires a lifetime of treatment. Our codependent characteristics become habits and may be tendencies we lean toward for the rest of our lives."[1] But is lifetime treatment what *you* aspire to? What if you succeed in kicking those habits and changing your ways? Why should you keep going for treatment, keep dwelling on problems that no longer exist? Beattie insists that the Twelve Step program "works," but what she is heralding is enforced dependency, not recovery.

By comparison, imagine that you were meeting a therapist for the first time and he told you, "I will work wonders for you—but only if you will meet with me at least once a week for the rest of your life." I have known therapists to warn patients that it may take several years to unravel their problems, but I have never met a psychologist or psychiatrist who associated lifetime treatment with recovery. On the contrary, most therapists consider the concepts of recovery and lifetime treatment to be mutually exclusive.

The point is not that you should completely reject Twelve Step programs, but that whatever form of therapy you choose should serve your personal needs and not vice versa. If there is not a "good fit" between the treatment and the problem, you are not likely to make much progress. For this reason, I am always wary of therapists who identify themselves as specialists in a single approach, such as psychoanalysis or humanistic, behavioral, or family systems therapy. Each of these approaches is useful in dealing with certain problems and certain kinds of people, but no single approach works for every situation, and most people are best served by a combination of therapies. This is especially true of addictions, which usually mask several different social, environmental, and emotional problems, each of which may require a different treatment approach.

Before you begin the selection process, then, you need to ask yourself exactly what you want out of the therapeutic process. Do you want a short-term fix or long-term solutions? Are you ready to learn how to cope with your own problems and prevent their recurrence, or do you just want someone to tell you that your problems are not your fault? Do you want your treatment to challenge you to get better or to collude with you in your victimization?

The approach that challenges you to get better is a bit like surgery or chemotherapy as a treatment for cancer: it may make you intensely uncomfortable, perhaps even increase your pain for awhile, but it will push you to settle the problem once and for all. Collusion, by contrast, is the path of least resistance, the equivalent of an herbal remedy for cancer. It will make you feel good for the moment and may give you the illusion of strength through righteousness, but instead of freeing you from your problems, it allows them to linger and perhaps get worse. Like the cancer patient, you have a choice. Both options are available, and you may want to start with the less drastic approach as a way to ease into the process of change. It is important to remember, however, that the deeper you get into therapy of any kind, the more difficult it is to stop and change direction. For this reason, it's best to thoroughly survey your options before you enter any kind of treatment.

The following overview will give you a very general idea of some of the most common treatment approaches. This is intended only to orient you, not to direct you. Without knowing your particular problem I cannot tell you that one type of therapy will serve your needs better than another. But I hope this outline will give you a sense of the interaction that occurs in different treatment situations. Based on this information you can investigate the treatments that seem most appropriate for your needs.

TREATMENT OPTIONS

Counseling is often confused with psychotherapy, but the two are actually quite different. When you receive counseling, you generally receive some type of direct advice. Career and vocational counselors advise clients in making job changes. Rehabilitation counselors help clients to rebuild their lives after a traumatic loss or medical catastrophe. Crisis counselors guide clients through traumatic events.

One of the important functions of counselors is to help clients understand what's normal and what's not. When catastrophic events occur, this type of guidance can make a crucial difference in people's ability to withstand and cope with stress. As clinical director of the Beverly Hills Fire Department's Critical Incident

Stress Debriefing team, a postcrisis management service for the city's rescue personnel, I have seen the dramatic difference that counseling can make to paramedics and firefighters. When a PSA airliner collided with a Cessna over San Diego in 1978, no such program was in effect. Rescue personnel were expected to return to work as usual after the crash, and most did so. But many of them quit during the following year because they had no mechanism to handle their reactions to the disaster, no way of knowing that their anguish and confusion were normal. In 1986, however, when a similar accident involving an Aeromexico DC-9 occurred over Cerritos, California, the critical stress debriefing team guided the rescue personnel through the emotional aftermath, and few of the rescuers developed any serious problems or quit their jobs as a result of the crash.

Counselors generally receive far less training than psychologists or psychiatrists, and some receive no professional training at all. If you go into a neighborhood counseling center you may be counseled by a volunteer or student under the supervision of a licensed counselor. These centers are not set up to provide intensive, long-term treatment; however, they frequently act as referral sources for other forms of therapy.

Psychotherapy is a general term that covers a variety of approaches. The core difference between counseling and psychotherapy is that therapists generally work with the patient to change behavior through personal inquiry leading to greater awareness. There is less direct advice giving in psychotherapy, and more analysis of the patterns of thought and behavior that underscore the problem. Also, psychotherapy is practiced only by licensed professionals.

Psychotherapy can take several different forms. The patient may see the therapist one on one, or as part of a couple, family, or group. The patient's specific problems and goals will determine which is most appropriate. For example, if you have decided that you can no longer stand to be married and are determined to get a divorce, there's not much point in your going through couple therapy, but you may need some individual therapy to come to terms with your decision and the changes it will create in your life. If you've recently gotten divorced and are having trouble coping as a single parent, you might find family therapy helpful; if you are having trouble adapting to your new social life, you may be able to use group therapy to explore your new social identity and get feedback from others who are dealing with similar problems.

Encompassing these three different structural choices are a host of different theoretical approaches to psychotherapy. The following are some of the most widely practiced:

The psychodynamic approach dates back to Freud and his belief that abnormal functioning stems from traumas that occur during childhood, traumas that the adult represses. The focus of therapy, then, is on feelings rather than beliefs or behavior, and the goal of therapy is to change the individual's entire outlook and way of life rather than to resolve a specific problem. The original childhood feelings must be uncovered, acknowledged, and confronted for the analytic process to be completed. The process can take years and depends largely on the patient's ability to confide in the therapist and to retrieve memories and ultimately place them in perspective. It is frequently used with people who suffer from anxiety, depression, or neurosis but is not considered a useful treatment for more serious mental disturbances such as schizophrenia or for highly specific behavioral problems such as obsessive-compulsive behavior. One criticism of the psychodynamic approach is that it can give patients a great deal of understanding about the evolution of their problems without helping them arrive at any workable solutions.

Behavioral therapies focus on learned patterns of behavior rather than the thoughts or feelings that surround those behaviors. If the patient's primary complaint is a feeling, such as anxiety, the thrust of therapy will be to pinpoint how this anxiety affects the way the person behaves and then attack the anxiety by changing the behavior. Behavioral therapists use many different techniques to accomplish this end. "Systematic desensitization" conditions the patient to respond in a more acceptable way to the object of anxiety. If you were terrified of dogs, for example, the behavioral therapist might first teach you some basic relaxation techniques and then have you use the techniques to relax first around a stuffed dog, then when looking at dogs from a distance, and closer and closer until you are able to pet a dog. "Implosion" forces you to confront your anxiety head on and push past it, without the gradual approach; in the above example, you might be told to take care of a dog for three days or to volunteer for a weekend at the pound. Perhaps the most well-known behavioral technique is the one made famous by the national chain of Schick Centers for the Control of Smoking and Weight. Their "covert sensitization" treatments condition people to associate nauseating or painful imagery with the unwanted behavior. The use of mild electroshock, foul smells, and repulsive imagery in such programs has been criticized, but many people who successfully cure themselves of bad habits use this technique without even realizing it. The woman who keeps trim by associating sweets with a vision of herself as fat, unhealthy, and unwanted is using this method. So is the man who stops drinking because every time he sees or smells alcohol he thinks of the accident he had while drunk in which he killed a child. Behavioral therapy is sometimes criticized because it focuses almost exclusively on symptomatic behavior. However, when the behavior *is* the primary problem, it can be extremely beneficial. One advantage of the behavioral approach is that there are so many different techniques that it is possible to tailor treatment to the particular needs and problems of the individual patient. Behavioral techniques are often successfully used in combination with other therapeutic approaches.

• *Cognitive therapies* start with the assumption that problems are caused not by bad feelings but by irrational thoughts or ways of thinking. Cognitive therapists work with patients to identify false beliefs and change them. They often do this by directly challenging patients, presenting them with rational alternatives to their irrational ideas. For example, if you are depressed because you consider yourself a failure, a cognitive therapist might challenge you to identify all the reasons why you hold this belief and then challenge the underlying logic of these reasons, turning them around to find the ways in which they are irrational and may be preventing you from recognizing your strengths. Cognitive therapy has been criticized for focusing too intently on conscious thought and not enough on feelings or behavior, but, like behavioral therapy, it includes a vast array of specific techniques that can be fitted to the patient's individual problems, and it lends itself to the combination treatment approach.

Humanistic therapies, such as Gestalt and Carl Rogers's client-centered therapy, are based on the assumption that people are essentially good, and that problems emerge because we are prevented from reaching our true and full potential. Most humanistic therapists promise their patients unconditional acceptance as a means of fostering self-acceptance and self-awareness. Instead of challenging what the patient says, the humanistic therapist will often echo or mirror certain statements that seem particularly important or troubling to the patient. This is intended to prompt the patient to clarify these statements and possibly look into them more deeply. Humanistic techniques include role playing and projection to bring out hidden feelings and repressed conflicts. For example, to help you deal with a battle with one of your co-workers, a Gestalt therapist might have you face an empty chair, imagine that your co-worker is sitting in the chair, and say exactly how you feel about this person, what you think the problem is in your relationship. Then the therapist might have you switch roles, so that you are speaking for your co-worker. This forces you to see how others see you and may force you to confront aspects of yourself that you generally ignore or repress. The humanistic therapies have been criticized because they purport to be a kind of blanket treatment for all kinds of people with all kinds of problems, including serious physical illness and/or chemical imbalances, and because they do not always promote the coping skills and personal change that some people need to resolve their problems.

Drug therapy is used increasingly as an adjunct to psychotherapy for a variety of mental disturbances, including depression, anxiety, schizophrenia, and obsessive-compulsive disorders (signified by repetitive and irrational thoughts or behaviors that overtake normal functioning).

One relatively new antidepressant, Prozac, has been used successfully to treat such wide-ranging conditions as obesity, bulimia, obsessive-compulsive disorders, depression, phobias, and smoking addiction. Another antidepressant, desipramine, has been tested as a treatment for cocaine addiction, with a nearly 60 percent effectiveness rating.[2]

Many such medications have serious side effects and widely varying effectiveness. Critics of drug therapy argue that they provide only symptomatic relief, as opposed to psychotherapeutic approaches that attack the roots of problems.

Some advocates, on the other hand, argue that medication is the only way for some patients to attain the mental and emotional stability they need to utilize psychotherapy. Others maintain that some emotional problems are purely biological, and the only function of psychotherapy in these cases is to help the patient adjust to his or her newfound health after starting medication.

Studies that have attempted to compare the effectiveness of the two approaches suggest that drugs generally bring faster relief but that psychotherapy is equally effective after about four months of treatment and does more to prevent relapses.[3] However, for psychotic disorders such as schizophrenia, many psychiatrists believe that medication is an essential part of treatment.

Again, the critical factor is the fit of the treatment to the problem. Medication should be considered only if you have a problem for which a drug has proven effectiveness and you are willing to accept the possible side effects and the possibility that it will not significantly affect your problem. Despite the promising results of some drugs, there are still no chemical miracle cures for mental and emotional problems.

Self-help groups, like drugs, are widely used as a complement to traditional therapies, but unlike drugs they have largely been accepted by the mental health community without question or criticism. Many therapists send patients to these groups when they don't know what else to do with them. Others simply accept the groups as a good idea because the patients seem to like them. The prevailing attitude seems to be: Everyone says these groups are helpful, so why not use them? But with the proliferation of these groups, the unquestionable virtue of some self-help programs is finally being challenged.

On the positive side, self-help groups do provide social support, which people in crisis or emotional duress may not be able to find elsewhere. Members of large organizations such as AA and NA can attend meetings every day—and are expected to, during their first three months of recovery. And many self-help groups also match new members with sponsors who are available to them around the clock for phone conversation or personal dialogue.

Self-help programs provide clear boundaries and limits that may be vital for true addicts to arrest their behavior. But the majority of addicts are capable of eventually developing their own individual coping mechanisms and leaving the group. They do not require lifetime treatment. Ideally, self-help groups would tell members that they may stay in groups as long as they feel they need it, and would encourage them to develop alternative support systems and coping skills. Unfortunately, the groups do not send this message. All members are told that if they stop attending meetings they will relapse. And for many this becomes a self-fulfilling prophecy.

Ironically, the same features that make self-help groups so attractive to people in need can also be their most serious weaknesses. AA and other Twelve Step programs are aggressively nonprofessional and make a big point of describing themselves as organizations of, by, and for addicts. Group meetings are not supervised or monitored by any professional agency or authority, and group leaders are generally not required to have any special training in group dynamics or leadership skills.

This is a potentially explosive arrangement. Groups of human beings, regardless of their stated agenda, involve complex, sensitive, and potentially harmful interactions, which must be managed to protect individual members. Leaders of any type of organized group *need* special training to be able to:

- Monitor the impact of the stronger or more dominant members on the rest of the group
- Discern which individuals need special support or outside help
- Listen objectively to what's being said, without projecting their own problems or attitudes on the other members

- Mediate confrontations between members
- Protect the rights of individual members when personal or sensitive information is revealed in group

Leaders need to recognize that several powerful forces operate in groups. One is social conformity, or the tendency to downplay or suppress individual opinions in order to support the majority position. Individuals typically try to gain favor or other rewards and to avoid rejection or sanctions from the group. The power of group norms is so strong that we may make decisions we know are wrong just because everyone else seems to be making those choices. In one famous study, psychologists M. Deutsch and H. B. Gerard asked several groups to judge the lengths of a series of lines. The answers were very obvious, and no one in the group that responded individually made a single mistake. But in the other groups each subject listened to other people delivering incorrect answers before they made their own judgments. In these groups, the subjects averaged between six and seven errors apiece.[4]

In order to conform to groups such as AA, new members may allow themselves to be persuaded that their problems are much worse than they are, that they have completely different needs than they really have. In my experience, many of those who attend AA and NA are not truly addicted to drugs or alcohol. They may be attracted by the supportive atmosphere or the promise of help with a problem that they are willing to call an addiction, or they may be drawn in by the group's proselytization efforts. Once in the group, however, their natural impulse to conform can turn them into full-fledged addicts. People who have never actually been intoxicated may model themselves after long-term alcoholics in order to stay in the group. And group leaders who cannot recognize this basic group behavior will welcome these people, encourage them to view themselves as addicts, and as a result may intensify their long-term problems.

As strong as our tendency to comply with group norms is the tendency to reject those who deviate from the norm. Psychologists who study groups have found a standard pattern in the way groups handle deviant attitudes and behavior. At first the majority expend a great deal of energy trying to win the dissenter over to their position. But if these efforts do not succeed within a certain period of time, the majority give up and ignore the dissenter. After receiving more attention than normal, the dissenter ends up receiving far less than normal. If the dissenter persists in remaining in the group, he is likely to be punished in some way. He may be purged from the group, relegated to boring or menial tasks, ridiculed, or excluded from selective group activities.

Perhaps the most relevant findings for self-help groups have to do with the formation of "outgroups." Princeton psychologist John Darley has found that those who have been rejected or felt alienated in groups in the past tend to form their own groups with other deviants and are more heavily dependent on these groups for social support than those who easily fit into groups. The pressure to conform in these outgroups is actually higher than in most other groups.[5] This is an important point because people who turn to self-help groups frequently do so because they have been shut out of other social support networks. They often feel like misfits in their families, among their peers, or at work. One of the major attractions of these groups is that they provide a place where people with highly specific problems can gain that sense of belonging. But because they have experienced rejection or alienation from other groups, they are all the more vulnerable to these "rescue" groups. They are more likely to conform, more dependent on the group, and less equipped emotionally to separate from the group.

Self-help groups encourage this kind of substitute dependency. They also foster substitute addictions, as the ash trays, candy wrappers, and empty coffee cups in AA meeting rooms will attest. Program followers rightly maintain that it is better to be addicted to supportive people, cigarettes, caffeine, and sourballs than to hard drugs or alcohol. Sometimes a substitute dependency is necessary to wean addicts off their drugs of choice. But substituting one crutch for another gives a false, temporary sense of comfort and security. It does not alter the underlying patterns of dependency. It does not lead to self-reliance, and it can set up a relapse.

To understand how this type of substitute dependency can backfire, consider Hanna, a cocaine abuser who kept herself off drugs by attending group meetings every night. She felt happy, connected, secure, and confident of her ability to stay clean as long as her group reassured her each day that she was doing the right thing and sticking to her program. Her husband, Jim, who initially encouraged her to join the group, could not provide her with this same kind of reassurance, she said, because he was never a user and "didn't know what it's like." Gradually, Hanna became so enmeshed with the group that she closed Jim out of her life, and yet when he left her she felt distraught, unable to comprehend what she saw as his betrayal. Naturally she turned to the group for help and support, but instead of focusing on the marriage, they continued to focus on the drug connection, to blame Jim's codependence for the breakup of the marriage. The group's mission was to help Hanna with her drug problem, not to rebuild her marriage. Hanna became depressed and felt lonely and doubly betrayed. Her safety dependency had failed her. Unable to prop herself up any other way, she turned back to cocaine. This happened because the group—her treatment—had encouraged her dependence instead of equipping her to cope with her own problems.

Mutual support groups, as mentioned at the start of this book, do not attempt to fix, change, convince, convert, or even heal their members. They do not present themselves as a substitute for therapy or other types of treatment. They can serve as a beneficial complement to treatment, but their primary function is to augment social support networks—family, community, and peers—that may be fragmented or inadequate during times of crisis. Group is a safe place where you can admit your problems, your failures, and your feelings without fear of reprisal or judgment. It is a place where others will understand what you are experiencing because they have been through it themselves. In group, you know that you are not alone.

Mutual support groups are particularly helpful for people dealing with severe emotional crises such as critical illness, death in the family, or other personal disasters:

• In a 1986 study, University of California psychologist Morton Lieberman found that members of support groups for wid-

THE CODEPENDENCY CONSPIRACY

ows and widowers moved more rapidly through the depression and grief following the death of their spouses, and after several months they showed significantly higher self-esteem and life-satisfaction than bereaved spouses who received no group support.[6]

• Mutual support group participation has been shown to reduce the need for hospitalization among patients with emphysema, asthma, and bronchitis, and to cut by half the rate of rehospitalization among patients discharged from one state psychiatric hospital.[7]

• Men and women with rheumatoid arthritis who met for ten weekly support sessions facilitated by a psychologist showed greater improvement in joint tenderness than did a control group.[8]

• Women who had undergone mastectomy operations and who participated in a mutual support program called Reach-To-Recovery returned to normal activities sooner than nonparticipants.[9]

There are many similarities between self-help and support groups. Key differences are that mutual support groups do not impose a particular program or system of belief, members are not expected to make a lifelong commitment, and the group does not encourage proselytization. Additionally, many support groups are led or supervised by mental health professionals who are trained in group dynamics. This helps to mitigate against excessive conformity and individual dependency on the group.

THE SELECTION PROCESS

When you begin treatment you implicitly place your trust in the guiding program or therapist. Some approaches demand this trust as a condition for treatment; others earn it with support and insight. But even among licensed professionals, not all counselors, therapists, or group leaders deserve your trust. Many are more interested in following their own agendas—and holding onto you as a paying patient—than in answering your needs. Some apply the same form of treatment to every patient, regardless of individual need, which is a bit like a physician prescribing penicillin for every patient, regardless of the diagnosis. Unfortunately, the attention, support, and reassurance that most forms of therapy provide can be so seductive that you may not stop to question whether the treatment is appropriate in your particular case. For this reason, it's important to have one or two evaluation sessions before you begin any form of active therapy.

In the evaluation session, you will ask questions about the therapist's background, training, and treatment philosophy, and he or she will ask you to describe why you feel you need therapy.

Here are some specific questions you will want to ask:

• What kind of training and license does the therapist have?
• Does the therapist specialize in treating a particular type of problem?
• Does the therapist specialize in a particular type of treatment?
• What does the therapist try to accomplish through treatment—what are the treatment goals?
• How does the therapist determine what methods or techniques to use?
• How does the therapist measure progress?
• How long is the average duration of treatment in this therapist's practice?
• What approach or combination of approaches would the therapist use in treating your problems?
• How frequently would the therapist expect to see you?

I believe that a therapist who is willing to accept you for treatment without conducting at least one evaluation session is as unethical as a doctor who would operate on you without first taking an X ray, or a mechanic who would replace the brakes on your car without first testing them. No therapist is appropriate for every patient, no single form of therapy will work for every problem, and often the type of therapy you think you need may not be appropriate at all. I recently conducted an evaluation with a couple who had brought in their eight-year-old daughter for therapy. After two sessions, it was apparent that the problem rested not with the child but with the parents. They needed some parenting education and counseling. It would have been unethical for me to start the child in therapy, and it would have done nothing to resolve the family's problems.

My policy is always to recommend the least costly, least restrictive form of treatment. I would be suspicious of a therapist who told you that you needed daily sessions. Research has shown that five years of therapy twice a week produces the same results as five years of therapy five times a week. But there is a big difference in the cost of the two courses of treatment.

Remember that the ultimate goal of treatment is the end of treatment. The therapist who will best serve your needs is one who will challenge you to develop the self-reliance to *complete* the recovery process.

TREATMENT CHECKLIST

If you are shopping for a therapist or treatment program, use the following checklist as a selection guide. These suggestions will not steer you toward any particular treatment approach, but they will help to ensure that you receive the type of help best suited to your individual needs.

- The therapist or group leader has the training and experience to deal effectively with your specific problems.
- The therapist or group leader understands and respects your cultural background and values.
- The treatment approach is compatible with your basic values and beliefs.
- The treatment is tailored to your particular problems.
- The therapist conducts an initial evaluation of your case before beginning treatment.
- The treatment does *not* automatically focus on a single issue or problem (such as codependence).

- The treatment does not stereotype or label individuals as addicts or victims (e.g., codependents, AMACs, or ACAs).
- The treatment does not invoke God as therapy.
- The therapist or group leader is willing to challenge you, not just validate what you already feel or believe.
- The therapist or group leader does not advocate lifetime treatment.

NOTES

1. Melody Beattie, *Codependent No More* (New York: Harper & Row, 1987), p. 180.

2. John Goldman, "Neglected Weapon in Drug War," *Los Angeles Times* (April 6, 1990): 1.

3. David Gelman, "Drugs vs. the Couch," *Newsweek* (March 26, 1990): 42.

4. John Darley, Sam Glucksberg, Leon Kamin, Ronald Kinchla, *Psychology* (Englewood Cliffs, NJ: Prentice-Hall, 1981), p. 555.

5. Darley et al., p. 559.

6. Gregg Levoy, "A Place to Belong," *Health* (February 1989): 56.

7. Information from the California Self-Help Center, UCLA.

8. Louis J. Medvene, "Selected Highlights of Research on Effectiveness of Self-Help Groups," compiled for California Self-Help Center, UCLA.

9. Ibid.

CHAPTER 11

Develop Your Personal Strengths and Resources

It had taken two years of therapy and endless hours of soul-searching, but Melissa was finally divorced from her husband. She no longer feared Henry's tirades or yearned for his approval. She'd stopped agonizing over his sexual affairs. At last, she saw through his seductive hold on her and understood that his passion was nothing more than deceit. She refused to be his victim any longer. But, as exhilarating as her freedom was, Melissa's recovery was not complete. She had solved her problem but still needed to complete the transition to her new independent life.

At first Melissa resisted this idea. She assumed that she could simply erase the past decade of marriage, go back to the life she'd been leading before she met Henry, and start over. I pointed out that even if she could turn back the clock emotionally, which very few people coming out of divorce can do, merely starting over could lead her right back into another unhappy relationship. It was as if she had just had heart surgery and was debating whether to return to the sedentary lifestyle and high-fat diet that had caused her heart problems, or to a new, healthy regimen that might realistically prevent further complications.

Melissa needed to take stock of her values and behavior, then start building up her strengths and overcoming her weaknesses. She needed to develop resilience.

On the positive side, Melissa was extremely intelligent and thrived on her work as a landscape architect. She valued honesty, intimacy, accomplishment, and moral responsibility. She also had a large network of friends, established before she met Henry. These were all vital strengths.

However, Melissa had neglected or undermined many of these strengths during her marriage. Henry had consumed so much of her energy and attention that everything else got short shrift. She had lost track of many of her oldest friends and stopped talking to her brother because Henry didn't like him. Instead of developing her career, Melissa had cut back her hours at work to make herself more available to Henry. And, despite the value she attached to honesty, instead of challenging his lies or resisting when he asked her to join him in group sex and other sexual practices that repulsed her, she'd gone along, persuading herself that everything he did was an expression of his love for her.

Thinking that other divorced women might be a good source of support and advice, Melissa tried joining a self-help group for divorcées. She hoped to make some new friends, maybe gather some useful suggestions. Instead, she told me, she was enveloped by "suffocating sympathy. They were all so angry, they could hardly wait to dump on Henry and have me sob on their shoulders. But I'm not in mourning, and, although I feel a lot of anger toward him, I'm not about to devote my life to raging at him. These women talked of nothing but their ex-husbands. Even though they were divorced, their lives still revolved around their hatred of these men. That was exactly what I was trying to avoid!"

Melissa quit the self-help group after five meetings, but she knew that before she ended therapy she would need to build a network of people to whom she could talk openly about her problems and concerns. Finally, she began to reconnect with her old friends and family members and, after apologizing for abandoning them, gradually repaired the damage. In time even her brother forgave her, and when that relationship was mended she felt as if the continuity in her life had been restored. She was again part of a community of people who knew her, accepted her, trusted and cared about her. These connections were not unilateral, as she now realized her marriage had been, or blindly unconditional, as the self-help group was. Instead, they were fully developed, reciprocal relationships that balanced support with individual responsibility.

As Melissa renewed her social life, she found her interests expanding. She took up cycling and joined a cycling club, took a course in photography and began doing portraits of her friends. She was now accepting larger, more challenging landscape jobs but was careful not to go overboard and bury herself in her work. She knew that that could be as damaging to her health and stability as her obsession with Henry had been. She also wanted to leave room in her life for love and, one day, marriage again. Not an obsession based on romantic seduction, but an honest and genuinely loving relationship.

The hallmark of Melissa's new independent life, she decided, was balance. "I lost sight of my values once," she told me during our final session. "I'm never going to do it again."

Resilience is a vital part of recovery, because you can never be completely free of problems. There is no utopia. You will always face a certain amount of frustration, sadness, and anxiety. That's life. But the more positive strengths and resources you cultivate throughout your life as a whole, the fewer problems you will have in the future and the better equipped you'll be to handle those that do occur. If you have resilience, you can ride through these setbacks without letting them drag you backward. You may even be able to turn some of them to your advantage.

WHAT CONSTITUTES RESILIENCE?

One of the traits that most clearly separates resilient individuals from chronic victims and addicts is that resilient people define themselves by what they *can* do while others tend to define themselves by what they can't. They believe in their ability to control the general direction of their lives and are essentially optimistic. In this way, problems become challenges rather than insurmountable obstacles. Frustration and unhappiness are part of life, but not the primary ingredients. It's the proverbial "half full or half empty" argument. The glass that some would say is half empty resilient people call half full.

Resilience is not based on Pollyanna cheeriness, but on an honest appraisal of the human condition. No one is happy all the time, and yet the most unhappy people tend to be those who believe in and expect perpetual, unadulterated bliss. The more they strive for it, the more they are doomed to fail. The more they fail, the more disillusioned they become, and the more cheated they feel. Those who anticipate a shifting balance of contentment and discontent don't demand perfection. And even in the darkest situations, they usually can find positive opportunities.

One source of resilience is temperament. As Emmy Werner's study of children in Kauai indicates, some people are simply born with optimistic, easygoing natures that persist, even with abuse and misfortune in early life, and help them to become happy, productive adults.[1] Of course, this is great news if you were lucky enough to be born with these traits, but what if you weren't?

Fortunately, resilience has several other critical components that you can develop throughout your life: self-esteem, strong social supports, and positive values.

SELF-ESTEEM THROUGH SELF-EFFICACY

Self-esteem is widely regarded as one of the keys to mental health. High self-esteem breeds optimism, contentment, success, and general good health. Low self-esteem contributes to depression, unhappiness, failure, and addiction. Self-esteem is often described as a product of parenting, a character trait that is shaped and sealed during childhood. But, once we've accepted that our childhood is over and our parents no longer run our lives, what can we do to raise our self-esteem? Forever recycling the crises of youth will not do it. Developing a sense of competence and self-efficacy will.

Learning, helping others, mastering new skills and enhancing old ones all contribute directly to feelings of self-esteem. So does the positive feedback you receive for your efforts. But you have to give yourself permission to pursue and accept these positive rewards. It's easy to say "I can't" or "I don't deserve this," especially if you're still subconsciously trying to please a parent, teacher, friend, or lover who told you you weren't good enough. As long as your only objective is to please someone else, your accomplishments will contribute little to your self-esteem. That's why it is important to focus on challenges that are meaningful to you *regardless* of other people's reactions—challenges for which you can establish your own independent gauge of success or failure. If your efforts attract the attention and applause of others, so much the better. But the outside approval must be secondary to your own satisfaction.

Emmy Werner found that the most resilient individuals in her study were not necessarily gifted or especially intelligent, but they tended to have a broad range of interests and activities, and they made the best possible use of the skills and opportunities they did have. They developed hobbies or activities in which they excelled, and these provided them with both an escape from their problems and a sense of pride and accomplishment. They also valued education and achievement. Three-fourths of the resilient youths graduated from high school and went on to college, and by age thirty more than 95 percent, including the women who had young children, were employed full-time.[2]

As the Werner study suggests, one of the best ways to boost self-efficacy is to cultivate multiple interests and activities. Many people devote so much of their attention and energy to one pursuit—work, or fitness, or church, or nurturing others—that they develop tunnel vision and neglect the rest of their lives. Then, if and when they suffer a setback in their primary pursuit, they may be devastated because they have few interests or skills to fall back on. This is one important reason why substitute addictions so often backfire as a treatment method. Simply transferring an obsession with drugs or gambling or alcohol to an obsession with a substitute drug or self-help program does not achieve the balance of outlets and gratifications that is necessary for full recovery.

Achieving a balanced sense of self-efficacy, then, is a little like achieving a balanced diet. You need at least one infusion from each of the basic resource groups, preferably each and every day. These resource groups include:

Professional achievement. I am not necessarily talking about promotions, raises, and awards, though these can be very gratifying. The best measurement of accomplishment is the fulfillment that comes from doing work you enjoy, learning from your work, and doing it well *by your own standards*. With this type of achievement, you develop a sense of mastery and confidence that no outside award can give you.

Education and skills training. Too many people associate learning with youth. As soon as they leave high school or college, their ideas become fixed. Many never read a single book after they leave school, or learn any skills outside their chosen field. Then ten, twenty years later, they feel ignorant, dated, and inept. Knowledge is one of the finest sources of self-efficacy, and there is no age limit on acquiring it. In fact, adults over the age of twenty-five constitute more than 40 percent of all college students in this country, and women over the age of thirty-five account for nearly one-fourth of all female college students.[3] But school is just one form of education. Learning a new skill or researching a topic of interest on your own can give you the same jolt of satisfaction as taking a formal course. Each new bit of knowledge opens up new possibilities, new options, and reminds you that your fate is not sealed by your past.

Sports and hobbies. Again, most of us participate in sports and hobbies as youngsters, but drop them as time goes by. In later adulthood these activities may be even more beneficial than they are in youth. They provide valuable outlets for stress and creativity, and important lessons in cooperation and discipline. Shooting a basket, making a painting, or winning a set of tennis provides a strong ego boost, no matter what age you are.

Lifestyle strengths. The better your physical condition, the better you are likely to feel about yourself and life in general. Good nutrition, regular exercise, and relaxation all are vital for your physical and mental well-being. Additionally, physical fitness provides a unique sense of pride that contributes to your overall sense of mastery and self-efficacy. If you can conquer problems such as excess weight, high blood pressure, or chronic stress and fatigue, you are bound to feel more confident and energetic about resolving your other problems.

Ritual and routine. Our society has glorified disposability and mobility. We throw away everything from razors to automobiles, and nearly one-fifth of the population changes homes each year.[4] Yet all this transition only intensifies our common need for a physical and/or emotional center to our lives. A stable home, favorite objects or places, daily rituals, and family traditions can all help to center us, even when other aspects of our lives are uncertain or changing. Such personal anchors make us feel secure and stable. They give us a sense of continuity and control. And these feelings contribute to our faith in our own competence and worth.

Nurturance. Contrary to what codependence leaders would have us believe, taking care of others is not a disease. It is not a shameful or debilitating activity. It is a vital, human experience. People who cannot nurture, who care for themselves at the expense of all others are not healthy individuals. While it's true that some people become so preoccupied with others' needs that they lose sight of their own, the solution is not radical surgery but balance. Whether nurturing a child or spouse, a pet or even a garden, we all gain positive benefits from tending, caring, giving, and accepting responsibility for others. Researchers have found that men with loving, supportive marriages are approximately half as likely to develop heart disease as men in comparable physical condition who have less supportive marriages.[5] Studies have also shown that pets can increase health and morale, reduce blood pressure, and significantly lower the risk of death in their owners.[6] Nurturing life provides a sense of purpose that nothing else can give us. The pity is not that some people are overly nurturing but that others can't nurture at all.

Community involvement. Self-efficacy comes not only from the feeling that you can do a task well or that you have a sense of purpose, but also from the recognition that you are part of a wider community. Isolation and self-involvement can destroy personal confidence. Reaching out, helping others, working toward goals that improve the quality of life not just for you and your family but for others throughout your community, perhaps even for future generations, will give you this sense of belonging and meaning. It may help you to gain a better perspective on your own life to see it in the context of people both more and less fortunate than you. And community involvement may even benefit you physically. In 1988 the Institute for the Advancement of Health in New York City found that women who regularly volunteer to assist the handicapped or underprivileged frequently experience a "helper's calm" that can increase energy and decrease blood pressure, headaches, and body aches and pains![7]

Spirituality. Religious or spiritual faith can be a powerful comfort. It need not involve participation in an organized religion. Many people are more comfortable with their own private spiritual beliefs than with group worship. For others, however, it is important to be part of a community of faith. In the past, most children were guided into an organized religion at an early age. Today, many adults have abandoned traditional religions but are flocking to substitutes such as cults and self-help programs. The fundamental attractions are the same. Traditional religions and their substitutes all provide some sort of higher power or spiritual authority. They provide answers to questions of belief and behavior. They set forth certain rules and boundaries that their followers are expected to heed. But the values that traditional religions espouse tend to be family- and community-oriented rather than self-oriented. These include values such as charity, loyalty, and moral responsibility, which are glaringly absent from most substitute religions. Traditional religions celebrate history, and through history they try to provide a reassuring perspective on the mysteries of mortality and humanity. They are predicated on spiritual health, not disease. And most followers of traditional religions view faith as a source of strength and courage, not as a reminder of their own powerlessness. With the exception of some religious fundamentalists, most believers consider spiritual reflection to be part of their lives, but not their dominant function, and they do not generally confuse religion with medical or psychotherapeutic treatment. One of the real dangers of self-help groups and cults is that they encourage this confusion, making it difficult for followers to distinguish between recovery and worship. There is a distinction. If you belong to a self-help group, ask yourself whether your real interest in the group is social, therapeutic, or spiritual. If you are primarily attracted by the group's spiritual overtones, ask yourself whether your needs might be better met by a traditional religion than by a self-help group.

THE PERSONAL CONNECTION

Self-reliance is not the same as autonomy. Even the most self-reliant among us do not always function well in isolation. We need friends we can trust to love and support us. We need feedback and reassurance and respect. That we sometimes need to lean on each other for help and advice is all to the good. It may even be life-saving.

In a landmark study conducted in Alameda, California, researchers studied the social patterns of 4,725 people in 1965 and then tracked the number of deaths within this group over the next nine years. Those who lacked strong social ties—through marriage, friendships, or association with social, professional, church, or community groups—had death rates up to three times higher than those with strong social support systems. Marriage provided the greatest protection for men, and close personal friendships were most important for women. Membership in groups seemed to provide the least protection.[8]

The tragedy in our culture is that so many people are forced to rely on groups as their primary source of social support. Increased rates of divorce, crime, relocation, and urbanization have all helped to fragment the tightly knit family and community structures that characterized much of American life through the first half of this century. Today it is not at all uncommon to meet men and women who refuse to speak to their own parents or children, who refuse to open the door to their neighbors, who cannot name a single person whom they trust implicitly. And yet, perversely, these are often the very same people who, in the perceived safety of a self-help group, will tell complete strangers the most intimate, darkest details of their lives. These groups offer the emotional shelter that their members crave. But the craving is not necessarily rooted in pathological flaws, addiction, or disease. Many of those who "need" self-help groups do not need treatment but community. They are not sick but socially starved.

Years ago, I worked at Children's Hospital in Los Angeles in a program for the families of physically abused and neglected children, who were referred to us through the courts. Many of our clients were poor, undernourished, with little education and few financial or social resources. The program provided them with parent education and physical and psychological treatment for both parents and children. We also held social events, including a weekly dinner and holiday parties, at which they could meet and talk informally with each other and staff members. The program was so popular that several of the clients described it as the best thing that had ever happened to them, and pretty soon word spread to other people in their communities. One day a young woman appeared with her two young daughters in tow. New to Los Angeles, she had no friends and few resources. She had heard about the program from a woman waiting for a bus and knew that it was restricted to abusive parents and their children. "I abused my kids!" she told me. "I want to be in your program." Of course, she had never abused her children, and it took only a few minutes to figure out that what she really needed was some guidance to the local community services and some suggestions for ways to plug into a positive community of people. But she was so desperate, her feelings of isolation and social alienation so acute, that she'd been willing to call herself a child abuser in order to find some friends.

At Children's Hospital we would not accept families into our program without evidence that abuse or neglect had occurred, but had this woman turned up at a codependence group she would have been admitted without question. And the rescue and support she received would have had long strings attached. She probably would have become convinced that she had an incurable disease. She would have been encouraged to recruit new members. She would also have been encouraged to treat the group as her primary source of social and emotional support rather than as a transitional resource.

Emmy Werner's research suggests that resilient people develop constructive relationships to replace or counterbalance dysfunctional ones. Despite coming from abusive, divorced, or alcoholic families, the resilient subjects in her study had close, trusting relationships with other people throughout their lives. If their parents were unavailable or abusive, they adopted other relatives, siblings, regular babysitters, or neighbors as substitute parents. In school, they tended to have at least one close friend, and usually several, including both peers and elders who could counsel them during periods of crisis and change. Most had a favorite teacher, youth leader, or minister who served as a role model and confidant. They also strengthened their social skills by participating in cooperative activities, such as sports, musical groups, or hobby clubs, where they learned that they could depend on their teammates—and vice versa. "With the help of these support networks," writes Dr. Werner, "the resilient children developed a sense of meaning in their lives and a belief that they could control their fate. Their experience in effectively coping with and mastering stressful life events built an attitude of hopefulness that contrasted starkly with the feelings of help-lessness and futility that were expressed by their troubled peers."[9]

ADDICTION, VALUES, AND DISEASE

The leaders of the Twelve Step movement suggest that addiction overpowers us, causing us to behave and think in ways that are inconsistent with our personal values. Nothing could be further from the truth! Addictions do not undermine personal values, they *reflect* them. The Irish alcoholic's culture teaches him to value intoxication and the act of drinking more than he values moderation or sobriety. Certainly he feels conflict, but that conflict is not between some phantom addiction and his own good values, it's between the two sets of values that reside within himself. One set tells him that he's not a real man if he can't keep up with his drinking buddies, and the other shames him when he gets so drunk he can barely function. Without read-justing these values, he can never completely recover.

As long as we conceptualize addictions and other bad habits as forces outside ourselves we will never gain control of them. The only way to overcome them is to work from within, con-fronting our negative values and enhancing our positive ones.

Of course, tinkering with values can be risky. Trying to simply invert them, as fundamentalist religions and Twelve Step pro-grams do, is often counterproductive. The fundamentalist ideal is to turn a sinner into a saint through the mechanisms of public confession, repentance, and spiritual rebirth, after which the sinner will feel such shame whenever he even thinks of erring that he will bend over backward to do good. The Twelve Step programs use an almost identical strategy to turn addicts into abstainers. The theoretical basis for this strategy is what psy-chologists call reaction formation. This is the process by which instinctual desires are turned into their opposites. Freud noted this phenomenon in patients who were so shamed by their sexual desires that they unconsciously turned the object of desire into an object of revulsion. In this way, wrote Freud, a young man looking at an attractive young prostitute would see her as a haggard old nun. When used as an antidote for addiction, reaction formation turns the addict's elixir into a poison.

The problem with reaction formations is that they suppress the negative value without changing it. That's like putting a lid on a volcano. The heat and pressure keep building up under the lid until, sooner or later, the volcano blows. And, after it blows, it may be impossible to get the eruption back under control. The same thing happens with instinctual desires or deep-seated values that we try to hoodwink. Sooner or later, the old desires are likely to break through, and when they do they take on new, exaggerated dimensions. After studying alcoholics from a variety of programs, including AA, George Vaillant concluded that rigid abstinence tends to attach such shame and fear to the act of drinking that even a minor lapse will produce feelings of intense failure, which in turn tend to trigger full relapse: "Once adherence to a rule of absolute abstinence is broken, previously sober alcoholics often find it enormously difficult to return effectively to a program."[10] In other words, when alcoholics resort to imposed abstinence *without changing the relative value of drinking in their lives*, they intensify their inner conflict and may reduce their prospects of long-term recovery.

How do we know that such relapses are caused by distorted values and not by some physiological reaction to alcohol? Because alcoholics who drink alcohol *without knowing* that it's alcohol do not relapse. In an experiment designed by psychologist Alan Marlatt, one group of alcoholics was given heavily flavored alcoholic beverages and led to believe that they were alcohol free. Another group was given nonalcoholic beverages and told that they contained alcohol. The alcoholics who drank the least were the ones who drank alcohol unknowingly. Those who thought their drinks contained alcohol drank to excess. The alcoholics' behavior was driven not by physical disease or chemistry but by the value they associated, consciously or subconsciously, with the consumption of alcohol.[11]

Surveys comparing obese people who lose and then regain huge amounts of weight with others who maintain their lower weight also support the values vs. physiology argument. As with alcoholics who attempt abstinence, overeaters who crash diet have a high relapse rate—some estimate it as high as 90 percent. They are three times more likely to regain their weight than those who lose more slowly. One explanation may be that crash dieting seems to change the body's metabolism so that it takes fewer calories to gain weight afterward. Another explanation is that crash and liquid dieters develop a reaction formation against food, so that when the diet ends and they return to eating, they are more likely to binge and keep on bingeing.

But these possibilities do not explain the success of dieters who keep their excess weight off. The explanation for that has far more to do with values and attitude than biology. When people come to value health, fitness, and moderation more than impulse gratification, they can adopt the exercise and dietary habits that will keep them thin for life. When they do not make this shift but keep trying to suppress their basic values instead of changing them, they are setting themselves up for failure. *Newsweek*'s overview of the liquid diet craze summed up this essential dilemma:

> Biochemically or behaviorally, the fight against fat is harder for some people than for others. Life isn't fair. They have to decide if struggling into a more pleasing shape is worth a lifetime of supreme self-control. Maybe it isn't. America loved Oprah Winfrey, after all, long before she was a size 10. But if keeping weight off is important enough, the method for losing it— whether it's a quick fix or a long haul—really doesn't matter.[12]

How do we go about changing negative values into positive ones? Instead of pouring all our energy into trying to suppress what cannot be suppressed, we need to start by accepting the negative, acknowledging that we have certain weaknesses, and then reducing their relative power over us by developing more positive attitudes, beliefs, and priorities. We have to adjust the balance so that our constructive values outweigh our destructive ones. The man who cares a great deal about the welfare of his family, the progress he is making at work, and the quality of his marriage, and who is only moderately attracted to the chemical high of cocaine is not likely to become a cocaine addict unless he allows the balance of his values to shift. If this balance does shift and he comes to prize his high more than his family and career, then he won't be completely free of his drug habit until his shifts the balance back in favor of his positive values. The important thing to realize here is that he knows and acknowledges that he enjoys the drug. He doesn't try to delude himself that he hates it or doesn't want it. He recognizes that when he uses, he is *choosing* to use. But when he is completely recovered, he also knows that the only choice that is consistent with his values is to remain clean, and, because his values are strong enough, that's the only choice he'll accept.

Certain values have a protective effect on us. They provide comfort and faith, confidence and courage. They help us to accept ourselves and others. They serve as anchors during periods of difficulty or confusion. They are sources of conscience and common sense. They give us the strength to tackle our problems and ask for help when we can't cope on our own. They give us a sense of meaning and hope. By cultivating these protective values, we enhance the quality of our lives:

- Mastery of a broad range of knowledge and skills
- Self-awareness and the ability to criticize ourselves without condemnation or blame
- An optimistic view of the world
- Faith in our ability to continually develop and improve ourselves
- A sense of personal responsibility for our actions and beliefs
- Respect for ourselves and others
- Emotional intimacy with at least one other person
- Concern for others in the community and society

In the end, the best thing we can do to ensure our well-being is to recognize the value of our own lives and the lives of others, and to do everything within our power to enhance the quality of those lives.

YOUR PERSONAL INVENTORY OF STRENGTHS AND RESOURCES

You develop personal strengths and resources throughout your life. This development is an ongoing process, and is the one part of recovery that does continue after you are fully recovered. The constant renewal of these strengths is not a chore or a duty, however. It is your greatest source of pride.

How strong are your personal strengths? To find out, answer the following questions according to this scale:

1 = Never
2 = Rarely
3 = Sometimes
4 = Often

Professional achievement

_____ Do you feel proud of the quality of your work?
_____ Do you spend extra time on a project because it genuinely interests you?
_____ Do you learn new information or skills in the course of your work?

Education and skills

_____ Do you read books that have nothing to do with your work?
_____ Do you attend educational courses, workshops, or lectures?

_____ Do you practice old skills, such as foreign languages, math, or music, even though you don't use them any more?

Sports and hobbies

_____ Do you practice a sport?
_____ Do you engage in any creative hobbies, such as cooking, painting, writing, or gardening?
_____ Do you participate in any hobby groups or clubs?

Lifestyle strengths

_____ Do you eat a balanced diet?
_____ Do you exercise three or more times a week?
_____ Do you get enough rest and relaxation?

Ritual and routine

_____ Do you follow a regular daily schedule?
_____ Do you see or talk with old friends?
_____ Do you engage in family rituals or traditions (holiday celebrations, birthdays, anniversaries, reunions)?

Nurturance

_____ Do you spend time taking care of another living thing (person, animal, or plant)?
_____ Are you willing to help other people without expecting repayment?
_____ Do you accept responsibility for the members of your family (children, spouse, parents)?

Community

_____ Do you participate in community events (school, neighborhood, or church/temple gatherings)?

_____ Do you engage in any volunteer activities?

_____ Do you participate in any political, social, or environmental action groups?

Spirituality

_____ Do you attend a church or temple?

_____ Do you pray or meditate?

_____ **Total your responses here.**

Looking back over your answers, you can identify your greatest strengths by finding the areas with the most 4s. For example, if you replied with three 4s under the category of lifestyle strengths, then health and fitness are positive resources for you. If you replied only with 1s and 2s in certain categories, then you probably need to devote more energy in those areas. Review this chapter for suggestions that can help you increase your resilience and self-esteem.

To measure your overall resource level, compare your total score with the ratings below:

23–46: Your resources are relatively weak. To maintain your self-reliance, you will need to devote more time and attention to boosting your personal strengths and becoming more involved with the people around you.

47–69: You have relatively strong resources but could develop them more. You may be concentrating too heavily on one area of your life and neglecting others. Try to achieve more of a balance.

70–92: You have extremely strong resources that will help you to sustain your self-reliance. Keep up the great work!

Whatever your scores today, remember that your strengths and resources are constantly changing. Just as your body needs constant care and feeding to stay healthy, so does your mind. So do your emotions. So does your behavior. This personal maintenance is an ongoing process. It is not just part of recovery. It is part of life.

NOTES

1. Emmy E. Werner, "High-Risk Children in Young Adulthood: A Longitudinal Study from Birth to 32 Years," *American Journal of Orthopsychiatry* (January 1989): 72–81.
2. Ibid.
3. Bureau of the Census, *Statistical Abstract of the United States 1988* (Washington, D.C., 1987), pp. 140–41.
4. Ibid., p. 20.
5. Walt Schafer, *Stress Management for Wellness* (New York: Holt, Rinehart and Winston, 1987), p. 211.
6. Ibid., p. 216.
7. Allan Luks, "Helper's High," *Psychology Today* (October 1988): 39–42.
8. Schafer, p. 210.
9. Emmy E. Werner, "Children of the Garden Island," *Scientific American* (April 1978): 106–11.
10. George Vaillant, *The Natural History of Alcoholism* (Cambridge, Mass.: Harvard University Press, 1983), p. 203.
11. G. A. Marlatt, B. Demming, and J. B. Reid, "Loss of Control Drinking in Alcoholics: An Experimental Analogue," *Journal of Abnormal Psychology* 81 (1973): 223–41.
12. Melinda Beck, "The Losing Formula," *Newsweek* (April 30, 1990): 58.

What It Means to Be Recovered

Freeing yourself was one thing; claiming ownership of that freed self was another.
—TONI MORRISON
Beloved

How can you tell when you are truly recovered? How can you be sure that your old habits won't creep back and overtake you? According to the Twelve Step gurus, the answers to these questions are painfully simple: you can never tell when you're truly recovered because complete recovery is an impossible dream, and you can never trust that your old habits are gone because they can *always* come back to haunt you. Anyone who claims otherwise, they say, is in denial.

I do not suggest that recovery is simple, but neither is it impossible. If you have followed the suggestions in this book and they have worked for you, there is a very good chance that your recovery is at hand. How can you tell if and when it's safe to stop doubting your well-being? One way is to check your current attitudes, behavior, and beliefs against the following hallmarks of recovery.

1. You no longer engage in the problem behavior. This is the most obvious criterion for recovery. If you smoked five years ago and have not had a cigarette since, then you probably do not have a smoking problem anymore. If you dieted and purged in college but have eaten normally and maintained a normal weight for the ten years since you graduated, then you no longer have an eating disorder. And if you've quit falling in love with people who betray you and have established an equal, honest, and loving relationship with someone who makes you genuinely happy, then you will probably do better to concentrate on developing the positive aspects of this relationship than to keep inspecting it for traces of codependence. Give yourself credit. It's just possible that you really have recovered!

2. You no longer crave the problem behavior. Conquering the craving is usually far more difficult and takes much longer than simply stopping a problem behavior. Most cravings mask an underlying need for something other than the problem behavior. A child who craves candy may need calories because he is not eating enough nutritious foods, or he may use candy as a consolation for feelings of rejection or failure at school. A woman who craves expensive jewelry may need reassurance of her value and worth. One function of the recovery process is to identify and satisfy the hidden needs, while replacing unhealthy values, such as greed, with healthy ones, such as appreciation and moderation. Once those hidden needs are fulfilled the craving will subside. The child may still like candy but is now satisfied by an occasional chocolate bar, and the woman may still love to look at quality jewelry, but she no longer is obsessed with possessing it.

As I've said, this aspect of the recovery process is not always quick and easy. There are alcoholics who, even after ten or more years of sobriety, still have to fight the craving for alcohol. I would generally agree with AA that these alcoholics are recovering, and not fully recovered. But many, if not most, of the alcoholics who have remained sober for that length of time do not continue to crave alcohol. They no longer desire the "buzz" of intoxication. They're not interested in losing control. Their values and priorities have shifted so that there is no longer room in their lives for alcohol. They have achieved complete recovery.

3. Your thoughts and conversations are no longer dominated by the same recurrent problems. When you have serious problems and when you are actively working to resolve those problems it is natural to become preoccupied with them. You may need to talk about them. You may wake up in the middle of the night, worrying about them. You may have difficulty concentrating on anything else. But as you move toward complete recovery, this preoccupation will gradually fade. Your attention will turn to other issues, other pursuits. Your conversations will open up to encompass ideas and experiences that bear no connection to your past problems.

A funny thing can happen when you reach this point in recovery. You may find it difficult to remember what you are recovering from. Intellectually, of course, you know that you had a chemical dependency or bad marriage, were overweight or depressed. But if the problem no longer owns you, then you are free to disengage from it emotionally. And when you hear people commiserating about the same traumatic experiences that once ruled your life, you may have difficulty identifying with them. This does not mean you're in denial. It means you're recovered.

4. You are not hooked on substitute addictions. As I stated at the outset of this book, being free of addictions does not mean that you are free of dependencies. Certain dependencies are normal and healthy. Eating, drinking, loving, thinking, caring, helping, working, sleeping, nurturing, and creating all fall into this category. These basic needs are what make you human. They provide the foundation for many of your most positive values. But addictions distract you from these core dependencies and alter your values. They prevent you from moving ahead with your life. Like a revolving door, they keep you in motion, going nowhere. Substitute addictions may change the pattern or speed of rotation, but the net result is the same.

In my opinion, the former crack addict who has been clean for three years but now chain smokes and attends daily Twelve Step meetings is not recovered. He has simply replaced his addiction to narcotics with addictions to nicotine and his program. If these substitutes were withdrawn, he would probably return to drugs because he has not established enough internal coping and problem-solving mechanisms to satisfy his healthy dependencies. Only when the substitutes are withdrawn and he succeeds in achieving a normal life without artificial crutches can he consider himself fully recovered.

5. You no longer blame your past problems for current mistakes, frustrations, or disappointments. Complete recovery means having the strength and confidence to face each situation as it comes, without constantly using your past problem as an excuse or scapegoat. If you're having problems in your marriage now, you don't automatically blame it on the cocaine habit you had as a teenager. If you have just lost your job, you don't assume that it's because your parents denigrated you thirty years ago.

Even if there is a connection between previous and current problems, you need to recognize that your primary task is to deal with the present. Understanding what's gone wrong before is important to prevent you from repeating past mistakes, but the only way to create positive change is by accepting responsibility for your life now.

6. You no longer need problems to make you feel special or unique. Complete recovery means having enough faith in your own essential value that you do not need to adopt your problem—your "disease"—as your identity and badge of honor. You do not feel compelled to describe yourself as a problem person to attract other people's interest or sympathy. You understand that labeling yourself as an addict, victim, or codependent is not the best way to get attention.

When you have recovered, you realize that your specialness is created and re-created in each day's thoughts, feelings, and actions, that you are lovable because of the way you connect and care about others, and that you are valuable not simply because you have survived, but because you are involved in a positive, constructive way with the world around you.

7. Your social life no longer revolves around your problems. Shared problems can create powerful bonds between people, but they are not the healthiest foundation for relationships. Likewise, self-help groups can be socially seductive if you don't have other supportive relationships, but most are too narrowly focused to supply the rounded social life you need after recovery.

Healthy relationships are not based on pathology or pain. They are based on a free exchange of ideas and ambitions. They involve a broad range of interests. They require respect and understanding, but not necessarily agreement. And rather than simply reaffirming what we already know or giving us a forum for introspection, they help to expand our awareness, to challenge us to new possibilities, new discoveries.

8. You have the tools and awareness to prevent other problems from overtaking your life. In brief, this means that you are equipped to:

- Identify trouble spots when they are small and manageable. (You and your husband have recently begun to argue about the amount of money you spend each month on clothes.)
- Confront each problem directly and honestly. (You tell your husband that these arguments disturb you and that you want to work out a compromise arrangement before the problem escalates.)
- Assess the situation accurately. (You discuss the problem to make sure that the arguments are really about money, not dissatisfaction in other areas of the marriage or problems that one of you is having at work.)
- Match the problem with the appropriate response. (You work together to identify expenses that can or should be cut, and then you adjust your spending accordingly.)
- Recognize when you cannot handle the situation alone, and get the help you need. (If your husband refuses to cooperate but continues to bicker with you about your spending, you might ask a close friend or family member for advice. If this is not fruitful or if you have no one else who can help you, you consider seeking professional help.)

• Learn from your problems so that you can prevent them from recurring or, if that's not possible, deal with them more effectively the next time. (You develop the language to alert your husband to problems without accusing or belittling him, and enlist his help in working through solutions instead of simply making demands.)

9. Your life is in balance. The object of recovery is not simply survival but health and growth, a renewal of life in all its complexity. Being recovered means recognizing both your strengths and frailties, challenges and triumphs. It requires values, resilience, and a clear but broad focus, not tunnel vision. It demands balance.

When you are recovered, no single area of your life obscures the others. You are able to divide your time and attention among your personal interests, work, family, friends, and community. And you gain fulfillment from your positive involvement in all these areas.

10. You no longer view your life exclusively in terms of "one day at a time," but take things as they come, embracing the longer view of the future. When you are bogged down by problems, the future seems overwhelming—frightening and beyond your control. During the recovery process it can be very helpful to approach your life in one-day increments, focusing on the small, manageable challenges and gaining strength from the small, attainable triumphs. But, once you have recovered, the future no longer poses the same threat. While it is still essential to be alive to the process of daily life, to savor the present, it is also important to look outward and ahead.

You cannot take full responsibility for your life without envisioning and planning for the future, and you cannot be fully recovered without accepting that responsibility. This does not mean that you live for the future, but that you use the future, as you use the past, to inform your present life. You consider both the short- and long-term consequences of your actions before making decisions. You allow yourself dreams without pinning your hopes on them. You embrace the possibilities as well as the facts of life. In this way, you claim ownership of your freed self.

THE FREEDOM TO CHANGE

The self-help movement would have us believe that we are defined by our problems, which, in turn, are symptoms of our universal and incurable disease. I do not believe that human beings or the worlds they inhabit are nearly that simple. Nor do I believe that there is any constructive reason for people who have conquered their problems to keep looking over their shoulders for signs of their past afflictions.

When your problem no longer owns you, you are free to disengage from it. Life after recovery can and should be very different from your previous experience. You feel differently. You think differently. You act and function differently. And your outlook on the world is different. You are, in effect, a new person.

I have many former patients who fit this description of recovery, but one of the best examples is a personal friend who heard me talking about this book and shared his own story with me.

I have known Larry for years as one of the most respected physicians in Los Angeles, a dedicated husband and father, and a loyal friend. He is also a gourmet cook and connoisseur of fine wines, and he loves to entertain. I knew that Larry was from Chicago and that he'd worked his way up from a lower-middle-class background. I had no idea that he'd dropped out of high school at age sixteen and become a heroin addict.

"If I walked into AA today," he said, "they'd tell me I'm still an addict. And I'm telling you that's crazy. It was another lifetime."

Larry's addiction was a product of his environment. He grew up on the streets, in a tough neighborhood with a broad ethnic mix where fighting was a basic requirement for survival and organized crime was pervasive. Larry's father was a carpet sales-man, his mother a beautician. Larry, their fourth and last child, spent most of his early years trying to catch up with his older brothers. Before he was ten he was playing craps with them on the corner. By fourteen he was running numbers. When he became a drug courier he was making so much money that he decided school was a waste of time. But a year after he started shooting heroin the money ran out and he realized he was at a dead end.

Larry checked himself into a rehabilitation program. Based on a confrontational model rather than the Twelve Steps, it prompted him to see how his addiction had developed and how he would have to change his thinking and behavior to keep from relapsing. When he completed the program, Larry moved out of the neighborhood and away from his brothers. He got a job as a clerk in a men's clothing store and began night school. Over the next ten years, as he completed college and medical school and moved to the West Coast, he rarely looked back to his troubled period. Now, almost no one outside his family knows that he ever used heroin.

"Why advertise it?" he asked after telling me the story. "I'm not a stupid kid anymore. I still remember what the stuff did to me and that's enough to ensure that I'd never touch it again. But if I told my patients that I was once an addict, a lot of them would leave me. If I told my colleagues, they'd start to question my judgment. If I told my friends, I'd never hear the end of it.

"You know, Stan," he continued, "I'm not proud that I was an addict, but I'm not proud of my recovery either. It was something I had to do to survive, that's all. On the other hand, I *am* proud of my marriage, my kids, and my career. I want to be judged for the positive things I'm doing today, not for something that happened three decades ago.

"Alcoholics Anonymous and all these self-help groups that are so popular right now have turned addiction into a kind of elite club, and once you're in you can never get out. I don't need that kind of club to feel special." Larry paused. "I'm not sure anyone does."

THE POWER TO CHANGE

Being recovered does not mean being perfect or perfectly happy. We all have weaknesses, needs, and hungers. We would not be human if we didn't. But we also have the power to grow and change and heal ourselves, to move ahead with our lives. We do not all need self-help groups or Twelve Step programs. We can rely on other sources of support that are not predicated on affliction or dependence. And we can rely on ourselves.

In this book I have tried to give you confidence by guiding you to unexpected insights about yourself and your options. But no book can change your life for you. For words to make a real difference, you must translate them into action. You must change your own life, and you must learn to adapt as the changes take effect.

It can be done. You can rebuild your identity in a way that is healthy, happy, and sane. But, as you move beyond recovery, remember that self-reliance involves a lot of intangibles, such as intuition, instinct, courage, and trust. Have faith in your abilities and potential. Believe in your own essential worth. You have the power to change.

COMPLETING RECOVERY: AN EIGHT-POINT PLAN

1. Define your problems without labeling yourself.
2. Recognize the many different influences that have shaped your life.
3. Remember the past, don't live it.
4. Accept responsibility for your own choices and actions.
5. Focus on the goal rather than the process of recovery.
6. Tackle your problems one at a time.
7. Select a treatment program that nurtures self-reliance, not dependency.
8. Develop your personal strengths and resources.

Index

AA. *See* Alcoholic Anomymous
Abstinence, 17–18, 19, 48, 95, 97, 157, 208
Abuse. *See* Child molestation; Emotional violation; Wife abuse
ACA. *See* Adult Child of an Alcoholic Addiction
  boundaries of, 11–13
  broad usage of term, 3, 67
  celebrity revelations of, 46–47, 50–51
  character traits, 93–94
  development of, 8–10
  disease theory, 3–4, 6–7, 17–20, 44, 58
  incidence of, 126
  moderation vs. abstinence, 18–19, 48, 96–97
  pain/loss and, 127–28
  personal values and, 207–11
  and power to choose, 47–49, 125–29, 136, 207–8
  substitute, 181, 190, 217–18
  see also Problems; Recovery; Self-help groups; Twelve Steps; specific types
Adult Child of an Alcoholic (ACA), 17, 65, 68–69, 70, 88–89, 90
Adult children. *See* Inner Child

Adults Molested as Children (AMAC), 35, 38
"Aha" factor, 114
AIDS, 9
Al-Anon, 13
Alcohol abuse
  cultural influences and, 11, 95–97, 207
  disease concept, 17–20, 180–81
  moderate drinking distinguished from, 73
  motivation to change, 9–10
  obstacles to recovery, 144–45
  rates, 11, 126
  rehabilitation, 142–43
  relapses back to, 19–20, 97, 157, 167, 208
  and rigid abstinence, 17–18, 19, 48, 95, 208
  Twelve Steps' original focus on, 48
  see also Drunkenness
Alcoholics Anonymous (AA)
  and abstinence, 18, 19
  broad application of, xiv, 13, 44, 48, 150
  celebrity participation vs. original intent of, 50, 222
  disease issue and, 18, 20, 43

INDEX

Alcoholics Anonymous (AA) *(cont.)*
  group norms and, 189–90
  ethnic background and, 95, 96
  nonprofessional leadership, 188
  powerlessness aspect of, 47–48, 125–26
  problems associated with, xiii, 222
  relapses in, 19, 157
  rhetoric, 22, 53–54, 55, 60
  and self-sabotage, 167
  sponsor system, 55–56, 188
  voluntary participation aspect, 57–58
  see also Twelve Steps
Altruism, 59
Alzheimer's disease, 66
AMAC. *See* Adults Molested as Children
American Cancer Society, 7
Anger, 5, 89–90, 98–99, 168, 169, 197
Anonymity, 50
Antidepressants, 186–87
Antisocial tendencies, 94
Anxiety, 5, 149, 150, 165, 168, 179, 198
Attitudinal goals, 153

Balance, 210, 220
Bandura, Albert, 132
Barnett, Milton, 96
Barry, Marion, 12
Barrymore, Drew, 19
Beaches (film), 56
Beattie, Melody, 13–14, 16, 43, 180–81
Behavior
  attitudes and beliefs influencing, 77
  balanced, 220
  disease concept of, 3–24
  recovery from problem, 215–21
  recovery goals for, 151–52
  see also Addiction
Behavioral therapies, 184–85
Bill W. (AA founder), 50
Boggs, Wade, 49
Bradshaw, John, 16, 22, 40, 43, 51, 86, 87, 92
Bradshaw on: The Family (Bradshaw), 16
Brainstorming, 80, 158–60, 173
Bulimarexia, 8

Celebrities, 46–47, 50–51
Change. *See* Self-change; Recovery
Character defects, 21
Chiauzzi, Emil, 93–94
Child molestation, 31–39, 86
  categories of victims, 36
  divorce case issues, 32–35
  memory distortion and, 37–39
  and time distortion, 37–38
  treatment of survivors, 35–37
Children. *See* Adult Child of an Alcoholic; Child molestation; Family; Inner Child
Children's Hospital (Los Angeles), 205–6
Chinese culture, 11, 95, 96
Choice
  and myth of powerlessness, 49, 125–27
  power of, 127–29, 136
Cities on a Hill (Fitzgerald), 23
Clichés. *See* Rhetoric and rules
Cocaine addiction, 126, 187, 190–91
Co-dependence (Schaef), 66
Codependent movement
  basic theories of, 14, 15–17
  disease analogy of, xv, 16, 44, 66
  dysfunctional family emphasis of, 86–88, 97–99
  evolution of, 13–14
  flawed assumptions of, xv, 7
  growth and popularity of, 114
  leadership requisites, 50–57
  professional advocacy of, 50–51
  rhetoric of, 57–58, 60
  similar characteristics of members and leadership, 58–60
  women's insecurities as target of, 97–99
Codependent No More (Beattie), 16
Cognitive therapies, 185–86
Collective identity, 21–23, 48, 54–55, 57, 150, 189–90
Community
  recovery and personal involvement in, 203, 213
  self-help groups' appeal to sense of, 21–23, 219
Conformity. *See* Collective identity; Group norms
Confrontation, of past memories, 114–17
Contingency solutions, 163–64, 176
Control
  desire to exercise over others, 59

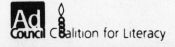